Why We Harm

CRITICAL ISSUES IN CRIME AND SOCIETY
Raymond J. Michalowski, Series Editor

Critical Issues in Crime and Society is oriented toward critical analysis of contemporary problems in crime and justice. The series is open to a broad range of topics including specific types of crime, wrongful behavior by economically or politically powerful actors, controversies over justice system practices, and issues related to the intersection of identity, crime, and justice. It is committed to offering thoughtful works that will be accessible to scholars and professional criminologists, general readers, and students.

For a list of titles in the series, see the last page of the book.

Why We Harm

LOIS PRESSER

RUTGERS UNIVERSITY PRESS
New Brunswick, New Jersey, and London

LIBRARY OF CONGRESS CATALOGING-IN-PUBLICATION DATA

Presser, Lois.
  Why we harm / Lois Presser.
    pages cm. — (Critical issues in crime and society)
    Includes bibliographical references and index.
    ISBN 978-0-8135-6259-9 (hardcover : alk. paper)—ISBN
978-0-8135-6258-2 (pbk. : alk. paper)—ISBN 978-0-8135-6260-5
(e-book)
    1. Crime—Sociological aspects. 2. Criminology. 3. Violence.
4. Violent crimes—Psychological aspects. I. Title.
    HV6025.P665   2013
    303.6—dc23
                                                        2013005975

A British Cataloging-in-Publication record for this book is available
from the British Library.

Excerpt from Thom Gunn's "Epitaph for Anton Schmitt" (1965) from
Selected Poems, 1950–1975, by Thom Gunn. Copyright ©1979 by
Thom Gunn. Reprinted by permission of Farrar, Straus & Giroux, LLC,
and Faber & Faber Ltd.

Visit our website: http://rutgerspress.rutgers.edu

Manufactured in the United States of America

For Ansel and Halen

CONTENTS

Preface and Acknowledgments

It's comforting to think that we are nothing like perpetrators of violence and other havoc. The distance allows us to identify with goodness and good people. I take the position that the difference is quantitative and not qualitative—that I have more in common with Pol Pot, Hitler, and the men at Enron than I might like to believe. I eat fish killed for this purpose, sometimes behave badly toward loved ones, and once kicked a moody roommate out of a low-rent New York City apartment leased in my name. Long before I began systematically investigating what I share with the worst doers of harm, I suspected that we shared many if not all of the same needs and desires— for respect, connection, and material comfort. Therefore I feel little regret in lumping harm doers together for the sake of analysis, as I do in this book. But lumping together harmful *experiences* is another matter. There is no comparing the harm of being laid off with the harm of having all members of one's family murdered. Victims are commonly treated as a homogenous group by criminologists and the criminal justice system; I am sorry to take a broad brush to their experiences as well. However, I collapse them in this book for the sake of discerning the logical systems that permit our harmful actions. I hope that the move to a general theory of harm ultimately amounts to greater recognition for and help to victims.

During research interviews, many practices that I thought of as harms did not get recognized as such by my participants. For instance, on the matter of killing animals for meat—"Is it harm?"—many speakers seemed not to understand the question. Were we asking if meat is bad for one's health? I take the business of lumping acts of harm together that do not seem to belong as a useful exercise in dismantling the fences we have built around them. Helping me to do so was a remarkable team of research assistants and supporters. Chris Belford, Leigh Dickey, Lori Farney, Amanda Greene, Rob Keeton, Lauren Ludwikowski, and Kurt Vincent assisted me with interviewing, transcribing, and analyzing data. Susan Silver was a wonder as copyeditor. Scott Frey supported me in a sabbatical, and Jon Shefner offered unwavering encouragement. Piers Beirne, Michelle Brown, Hoan Bui, Emily Gaarder, Bobby Jones, Rahim Manji, Jim Ptacek, Rachel Rich-Reynolds, Sveinung Sandberg, and Deb Sullivan provided invaluable guidance. To all of you who have tended to my children with love so that I could work (or rest), I am especially grateful.

Why We Harm

CHAPTER 1

Making Misery

ANGELA LEISURE LOST HER SON, Timothy Thomas, on April 7, 2001, after Cincinnati, Ohio, police officer Stephen Roach shot him to death in a dark alley. Roach and fellow officers gave chase after discovering that Thomas had numerous outstanding arrest warrants. Thomas was the fifteenth African American man killed by the Cincinnati Police Department in the space of six years, and his death galvanized many in the community to protest police abuse as never before (M. Singer 2002). The most sustained protest took the form of an economic boycott, launched in July 2001, whose purpose was to hurt the city economically and thereby force city leaders to respond to demands for accountability for the murder and to implement government reforms such as improved citizen oversight of the police. Joe Santangelo, promoter of Cincinnati's annual Jazz Festival, lost more than five hundred thousand dollars when that event was cancelled in 2002 due to the boycott (Nager 2002).

These two harms are markedly different from each other: one a killing perpetrated by state agents against citizens, the other a financial loss organized by citizens against commerce. Do they have anything in common other than their historical connection? I propose that certain deep and collectively shared logics pertaining to self and Other are common to both actions. These shared logics include a claim of occupational or moral warrant to do the harm, a declaration of having no nonharmful alternatives, and a reduction of the victim to a problem group—fleeing suspect or Cincinnati business.

This book is devoted to an understanding of the logics that promote human-instigated harm.[1] I can and do say little about the various actual experiences commonly linked with harm, variations on temptation, deprivation, and constraint or lack thereof. I take the view that experience is always already structured by interpretation. Some (most) aspects of "what happens" are always relegated to the background. My attention is on cause-and-effect relationships imputed to events, self, and Other characterized in particular ways. The relegating, imputing, and characterizing—and not experiences as they might conceivably exist prior to these cultural practices—promote harm.

I define harm as trouble caused by another. Harm differs from suffering or loss, which are its effects. The diversity of such harms and the intellectual puzzles that diversity creates inspired my analysis. Humans harm other living beings with alarming frequency in a variety of ways and have done so for as far back as historical records go. Harms include the sort of crimes typically handled by local police (e.g., murder, rape, assault, and theft) and the white-collar crimes handled by regulatory agencies (e.g., price fixing and insider trading). They include organized collective actions such as war, genocide, terrorism, torture, slavery, colonization, displacement, and human trafficking. Harms of political repression, such as election fraud, deprivation of civil liberties, the imprisonment of activists and journalists, and other abuses by state officials, like police brutality, appear to be common, although their documentation is unreliable. Other harms—including corporal punishment, incarceration, execution, abortion, environmental pollution, the manufacture of dangerous products, insults, discrimination, employee layoffs, sadomasochistic sexual activity, genital mutilation, enforced pregnancy, and animal flesh consumption—are regular events, although some are not regularly called harmful. Some harms, such as poverty, are not events at all, but rather states of being endemic to social structures, hence sometimes called structural violence.

We do harm out of desperation (e.g., fending off an attacker) and for entertainment (e.g., football). Many harmful actions are solutions to problems, and some such solutions do obvious good. The most successful surgical procedure cuts and thereby injures the body, albeit for a greater ultimate benefit to said body. Kill bacteria and you have caused harm to a living being. Even the most dedicated vegans are complicit in the extermination of microorganisms to nourish themselves. Still other harms have no obvious instrumental purpose, such as so-called senseless killing. Harms are premeditated and spontaneous, legal—even legislated—and illegal, conscious and unconscious. Harms include actions that are considered both mundane and shocking, and actions that are both praised and condemned. Harms include both taking action—firing a weapon, for instance—and failing to take action, such as neglectful parenting and tolerance of genocide. Agents of harm are individuals acting alone and groups such as governments, corporations, terrorist organizations, and gangs. Harm agents have vast resources at their disposal, and they are the most marginalized members of society. The victims of harm are people, animals, and the natural environment. The circumstances of harm are likewise diverse. I treat harm, for all its variety, as a unitary social phenomenon for the purpose of grasping the role of collectively held meanings in its imposition.

Theorizing Harm versus Theorizing Crime

From the outset it might seem that harms are too various to constitute a single phenomenon. In addition, the designation of some action as harm is subjective and context specific. I ask, though, do crimes hang together any better than harms? Crime includes loitering, homicide, marijuana use, and fraud. These actions are typically aggregated as crimes because they violate laws, but this is no more meaningful or stable a basis for grouping actions than is the fact of causing trouble.

Criminologists before me have recommended defining crime as social harm (see, e.g., Agnew 2011; Hil and Robertson 2003; Hillyard et al. 2004; Kramer 1985; Michalowski 1985). Paddy Hillyard and colleagues (2004) have called for an alternative discipline, *zemiology,* which is centrally concerned with social harm. I offer three reasons why I agree that harm is at least as worthwhile as crime as an object of study.

First, taking up the explanation of harm has a progressive aspect. Harm makes central a subject who gets harmed, whereas crime makes central either a criminal or the state. In the latter case the victim of crime is missing from the start, so an authority must define what crime is. To put it differently, definitions of crime and harm are ultimately in the eye of the beholder, but in the case of crime, the beholder is a governing, hence elite, body. In the case of harm, the beholder is its victim or an advocate of the victim.[2] As such, more harms get recognized more broadly when we focus our attention there.

A study of harm privileges the vantage of victims, and where perpetrators maintain more social power than victims do, this privileging can contribute to social justice.[3] Individuals hold different perspectives on harm depending on their social position and their relation to the harm. Most notably, victims are apt to call harmful what perpetrators and bystanders do not. An example is Jody Miller's observation that "girls believe sexual harassment is more harmful than boys do" (2008, 82; see also DeKeseredy 2011, chap. 1; Ni Aolain 2009). Whereas both crime and harm are problematic, the project of theorizing harm gets us away from the monopoly on definitions by the powerful, including but not limited to political authorities (Schwendinger and Schwendinger 1970).[4] Relatedly, I am pleased that there is as yet no ready word for an agent of harm, suggesting that no one has yet essentialized such agency. In contrast, the state of being an offender is now read off a set of events related not only to an offense but also to legal classification, scientific classification, and, not least, one's social position. If only for a limited time, a zemiology avoids the reification of harm agents.

Second, harm is at least as useful an analytic concept as crime because our concerns about crime are fundamentally concerns about harm (Shill Schrager and Short 1980; Sullivan and Tifft 2005). As such, harm is a more foundational object for explanation than is crime.[5] People are generally less inclined to endorse harsh punishment for crimes that do little harm (Cullen, Fisher, and Applegate 2000). What gets criminalized is that which caused or could cause harm—either to individuals (e.g., death) or to some collective—the social body (e.g., disorder) or a particular group (e.g., loss of profits). My heart is moved by the need to stop harm, but not always by the need to control crime. Past and present campaigns to control crime are themselves fraught with harm: they have truly been wars, with atrocities caused by fighters on both sides. In contrast, the effort to stop harm remains relatively untainted.

A third and final reason to theorize harm instead of crime is that doing so has the potential to shed new light on sociodemographic differentials in offending. Criminologists' well-established observations that young adults offend more often than older adults, that males offend more than females, or that most offending behavior targets persons of the same race and class are problematized when the offense is harm. Zemiologists are poised to uncover new patterns in the effects of gender, race, class, and age of both perpetrator and victim and on the extent and nature of harm done.

Leaving aside the scientific promise of the project of theorizing harm, what are its challenges?[6] I see two potential ethical problems related to theorizing harm instead of crime. One problem is that the emphasis on harm may enter into certain disclaimers articulated after the event. For example, James William Coleman reports on the neutralizations of white-collar offenders to the effect that they "did not harm anyone, and they have therefore done nothing wrong" (1987, 411), comparable to Gresham Sykes and David Matza's (1957) notion of denial of injury. I maintain that the prospect of such reasoning by actors ought not inhibit exploration by researchers. Indeed, the problem is not unique to the study of harm. Many perspectives on crime or concepts thereof can be adapted for use in neutralizations. For example, individuals take up the overarching paradigm of social science that posits human behavior as partly or wholly determined by social forces to excuse their misconduct. That tendency to co-opt the discourse of social science does not suggest that we should stop doing social science. We can and should distinguish between the statements made by harm doers regarding their past harmful action and those that precede their harmful action.

A second ethical problem with the project of theorizing harm is that it deemphasizes the role of intent. Whereas legal and social scientific definitions of crime generally require intent, definitions of harm do not (see also Pemberton 2007). I may cause harm without meaning to do so. Such harm is called negligent if I failed to take certain reasonable steps that would have prevented the harm. Corporate negligence causing harm to workers, consumers, and the environment and many so-called collateral civilian casualties in wartime are large-scale examples of unintended harm. Or, I may both deny intent to harm and deflect responsibility for harm onto a key collaborator. For example, makers of soda, tobacco, and guns sell products that surely do harm. Yet industry representatives point to consumer choice and behavior rather than these products as leading to the harm. When we say that humans act, we mean that they do something guided by intention or purpose. It follows that harmful action is guided by purpose, although that purpose is not necessarily to harm. It may instead be to amass profits or conquer an enemy. These harms are surely due in part to that single-minded purpose that occludes a view of all else.

Analysts of harm may reasonably study harms that are unintended and unforeseen, as long as the possibility of causing harm was foreseeable. The actors may not have intended to harm but they must have had some notion that their (in)action might result in harm.[7] We need not be concerned with the fact that actors' participation in harm was partial or "not all it takes," as is the case with the soda, tobacco, and gun industries: we can still analyze the part the actors in question do play.

Likewise, though perhaps more controversially, we may take *tolerance* of harm into the same theoretical consideration as we do the deliberate commission of harm. We daily tolerate harm in such forms as degradation of the planet, the torments that factory farming inflicts on the animals we eat, and injurious working conditions around the globe. The human actions behind these events could not be taken without the permission and the practices of bystanders. Principal among the necessary actions of bystanders is shielding themselves from awareness of harm. In doing so, they channel certain logics of self and Other, power and responsibility.

The Limits of "What Is"

From a general consideration of zemiology—the study of harm—I turn now to my own project of explaining harm in terms of cultural logics. Criminology offers theories of many, though by no means all, of the imposed troubles I have termed "harms." A short list of the dominant theories of offending by individuals and groups includes strain, control, learning, and rational choice theories. Relevant to larger groups and whole societies are anomie and conflict theories. Each of these theories links harmful action to psychological and social realities in the lifeworld of the harm agent or agents. Yet actors see the world through the lens of their own interests and experiences. Their realities look and feel different from those of the analysts and from those that are evident to the analysts. Mary Jo Maynes, Jennifer Pierce, and Barbara Laslett's critique of dominant theories of action serves equally well as a critique of theories of criminal action:

> What is missing is an alertness to, or more than a superficial interest in, key components of motivation: how individual actors come to understand their options, the varied meanings and orientations people take from their past experiences and bring into new situations, the components of their choices that are driven by emotions or dearly held values rather than by interests more narrowly or broadly conceived, and, at a deeper analytic level, how social actors understand their own capacity to act in a given setting. (2008, 23)

Criminologists are not inattentive to meaning making. They generally acknowledge that perceived reality is the key instigator of criminogenic processes. For example, social learning theorist Albert Bandura observes, "The notion that behavior is controlled by its immediate consequences holds up better under close scrutiny for anticipated consequences than for those that actually impinge upon the organism" (1973, 50). Yet most theories of offending connect objectively discernible events and circumstances with action. In presenting his general strain theory, Robert Agnew notes that strains or "adverse relations are whatever individuals say they are," but he advises scholars to conduct their empirical work on objective situations that the majority of people experience as strain (1992, 61). The demands of scientific assessment shape what we take to be the "real" causes of crime.

The sheer variety of circumstances of harm—scarcity and plentitude, anarchic and authoritarian societies—suggests that circumstances alone are not explanatory. To appreciate just how limited objective conditions are as motivators to action, consider the case of chemotherapy for cancer. The therapy, here, is a harm, albeit a harm with which the physician expects to achieve a greater good. Suppose that the chemical protocol is actually ineffective or even that no tumor exists. No matter: constructing the necessity of the protocol and the existence of the tumor in medical records directs the medical team to perpetrate the harm that is the chemotherapy. Those claims—and neither the actual effectiveness of chemo nor the actual existence of the tumor—motivate the physician to order this treatment. They galvanize the cooperation of other medical professionals, the patient, and loved ones and the approval of oversight agencies.

A sociopolitical example likewise makes the point that communication and not circumstance directs action. President George W. Bush's allegation that Iraq posed a threat to our national security propelled the U.S. invasion of that country in 2003. Critics of the president charged that Iraq was in fact never a genuine, imminent threat. Indeed, we would later learn that the allegation was backed by faulty intelligence. Observers call Bush's construction of Iraq, and the West's construction of Arabs and Islam, *ideological,* by which they mean, among other factors, that the constructions are false. Yet, as Philip Smith puts it concerning President George H. W. Bush and the first Gulf War (of 1990–1991), "Whether or not Bush and his supporters actually believed what he had said earlier about Saddam is beside the point. We need only understand that words are performative and that actors are held accountable to their rhetoric" (2005, 123). For the sake of theorizing harm we need not be concerned with the falsity of discourse. More precisely, we should be concerned with falsity only as a claim made in stories and counterstories.

The Role of Texts

Given the foregoing discussion, should we privilege *perception* in theories of human action? In my view, to do so would not yield a much more comprehensive theory of harmful action than one based on objective conditions. The main reason is that a perception-bound theory—one that emphasizes the way things seem to the actor—has difficulty accounting for harms perpetrated by aggregates. The amount of harm done evidently increases with the size of the offending party. For example, in 2007 more than five times as many Americans were killed by occupational hazards and disease—which is always, by definition, organized—than by firearms (Reiman and Leighton 2010, 88). How to gain purchase on such organized harms?

We ought not suppose that groups think or have purposes and motivations—that they are, in a word, agents (cf. Le Bon 1903). If a group can be said to think, as Mary Douglas (1986) proposes that institutions think and as Eviatar Zerubavel (1997) suggests in theorizing thought communities, then its thoughts are developed and maintained in some locale other than minds. Where might that be? The mind of the group—the engines and repositories of its meaning making—exists in its language-in-use. The way events appear to the members of a gang or the citizens of a nation is tied inextricably to the way they are communicated.

Returning to the aforementioned criminological theories, we ought to consider communicated phenomena about the proposed mechanisms as spurring group action. The reinforcement that the group has allegedly received affects group aggression. The informal sanctions that the group supposedly is at risk of receiving controls group offending. The constraints that the group tells itself it is under influences group deviance. And so on. If these revised propositions seem to imply cynicism, it is only because we are socialized to distrust what is said. Again, I am not concerned with the truth or falsehood of what is said; I am concerned with its role in behavior.

I have been critiquing mainstream criminological theories for overlooking the effects of discourse. But critical perspectives that emphasize the political economy of harm have the same blind spot. Consider the violence-promoting institutions that Steve Tombs identifies in his cogent argument against conventional codifications of violence: "the exchange of labour for a wage (paid work), the occupational structure, the uneven distribution of power within and around work organizations, the corporate form per se, the criminal justice and legal systems, and the state and its constituent elements, such as regulatory bodies and government ministries" (2007, 545). I propose that these institutions promote violence and furthermore are allowed to do so inasmuch as agents have constructed their victims as expendable and the structures as inexorable. Relative poverty, for example, is tolerated because of who the impoverished supposedly are and the alleged mechanism of the situation—the impartial, invisible, and unavoidable hand of the market. Even at the individual level, communication is causal. Pronouncing oneself as having a certain experience—say, as experiencing little power in a particular situation—is consequential. For we come to believe what we say, and we also manipulate conditions based on what we say and thus achieve outcomes that support our statements.

We come to believe what we say. Experiments based on Leon Festinger's (1957) theory of cognitive dissonance had participants write essays in which they took positions counter to their actual, prior positions on issues. The researchers later asked participants their positions on the same issues and found that people moved toward the position of their essay. Evidently they were influenced by their own communications. More fundamentally, what we think is constrained by what we are able to say. The Sapir-Whorf hypothesis captures this idea best. Benjamin Lee Whorf explained that "the forms of a person's thoughts are controlled by inexorable laws of pattern of which he is unconscious. These patterns are the unperceived intricate systematizations of his own language." Language provides "the forms and categories by which the personality not only communicates, but also analyzes nature, notices or neglects types of relationship and phenomena, channels his reasoning, and builds the house of his consciousness" (1956, 252).

But setting aside thought for a moment, we also manipulate conditions based on—usually to accord with—what we say. People talk themselves into action. To get in the mood for a fight, Curtis Jackson-Jacobs finds that "simply reciting a script of fighting words often helps to conjure the necessary emotions" (2004, 238). Leaders make claims and arrange matters to back those claims. In some cases their word becomes law. Even when it does not, they have the resources to disseminate a message and to dedicate resources to its realization. Moreover, they are held accountable for what they say. They need not believe in their claims. Attitudes often do, but need not, mediate the talk-action relationship at all. My theory is agnostic as to whether talk reflects belief. People do harm in part because to do so is all right in the culture, and they know it is all right because of prevailing discourses.

MISSING THE MARK

I turn now to discourses that engender harm. The tale of the hero fighting an evil foe for a greater good is particularly affecting. It justifies violence, but what justifies nonheroic harms that we also condone? Most theories of crime overshoot the mark when it comes to the small, thoughtless offenses. For instance, Jack Katz (1988) describes shoplifting and murder as enactments of coveted identities, but can the same be said of the mindless waste of environmental resources? Strain— frustration that provokes negative emotion (Agnew 1992)— seems a viable cause of assault, but what about speeding? What of harms apparently marked by nothing so much as

conformity and minimal affect, such as clerks rejecting applica-
tions for much-needed financial assistance, correctional officers
doing their job of caging people, and humans killing animals for
food or clothing? We see the mark of institutions in these practices, shaping views and vocabularies of what is possible and what
is permissible. Most general theories of crime, and theories of
violence in particular, were not designed to explain these unemo-
tional and unreflective harms and so are ill-suited to the task.[8]

Another observation grounds this project, which is that
criminologists have neglected government-backed harms,
most notably genocide (Day and Vandiver 2000; Hagan and
Rymond-Richmond 2009; Yacoubian 2000). Many blame this
neglect on mainstream criminology's reluctance to budge from
state definitions of crime. Certainly, we have made a fetish out
of explaining the sorts of actions regulated by official law
enforcement agencies. But neglected more generally, among
other things, is the hyperemotional, hyperactive character of
many instances of mass harm. The excesses of mass harm include
unthinkable atrocities—the destruction of bodies, the burning
of homes and fields, and "the extensive sexualization of violence
that is observable in nearly all the new wars" (Münkler 2005,
86). There is often a surreal aspect to the will to harm and degrade
reported in the accounts of witnesses and perpetrators. The will
to damage the bodies and belongings of others is often reportedly accompanied by specific affective states—repulsion and
rage (Young 2003) as well as gaiety and joy (Beah 2007)—
which must be but have hardly been reckoned with (see
Goldhagen 1996; Turner 2007; Wieviorka 2009, 92–96). A
theory of mass slaughter must clarify the will to destroy and not
just to seize, the will to cause suffering and not just to dominate.[9] Few scholars have attempted such a theory. Those who
have, agree that the nature of certain mass violence necessarily
entails a script concerning injustice vindicated or averted and a
strict differentiation of "us" and "them" (Gamson 1995; Hagan

and Rymond-Richmond 2009). Still, why violence? Why must blood be spilled?

HARM, EMOTION, AND REASON

Some scholars stress the emotional aspect of crime and violence (e.g., Agnew 1992, 2010; J. Gilligan 1997; Scheff 1994; Turner 2007). They tend to ignore, however, the fact that emotion is subject to discursive construction. We take cues from language, including metaphors, stories, and codes, on how to feel about circumstances and actions. We also take cues on which actions are compelled by which feelings. Pancrace, a Hutu killer during Rwanda's 1994 genocide against the Tutsis, described the managed yet rather flexible nature of emotions to journalist Jean Hatzfeld:

> The Hutu always suspects that some plans are cooking deep in the Tutsi character, nourished in secret since the passing of the ancient régime. He sees a threat lurking in even the feeblest or kindest Tutsi. But it is suspicion, not hatred. The hatred came over us suddenly after our president's plane crashed. The intimidators shouted, "Just look at these cockroaches—we told you so!" And we yelled, "Right, let's go hunting!" We weren't that angry; more than anything else, we were relieved. (2003, 219)

Some would locate the energy for the Rwandan genocide in anger, but anger seems not to have had a necessary, foundational role in the collective or even individual move to kill. Herbert Kelman concurs that "historical relationships provide a reservoir of hostility that can be drawn upon to mobilize, feed, and justify the violent actions, but they do not cause these actions in the immediate case" (1973, 37). And anger has no role at all in institutional harms such as the slaughter of nonhuman animals or the devastation of the earth.

Rational choice scholars agree that emotion is not central to harm. Rather than passion, the lure of gain motivates action that is calculated—cool, not hot. But rational choice perspectives minimize the role of discourse as well, codifying it as just so much talk or subterfuge. For example, Paul Collier notes that the true, economic reason for civil war often differs from the rhetoric, stating "even where the rationale at the top of the organization is essentially greed, the actual discourse may be entirely dominated by grievance" (2000, 92). He continues, "The true cause of much civil war is not the loud discourse of grievance but the silent force of greed" (101). I ask, though, What rhetorics permit us to act on greed or anything else? What rhetorics direct us to certain targets and not others?[10]

I discern the rhetorics channeled in *stories* in particular. Stories—or narratives—are a crucial type of rhetorical device for constructing who we are and what we intend to do.[11] We connect with general moral codes in telling our stories: the latter "provide social approval by aligning events with normative cultural codes" (P. Smith 2005, 18). The next chapter elaborates the particular role of stories.

How This Story Begins

This is what we know about harm:

- Harms are socially ordered, nurtured in and by institutions and other hierarchical arrangements.
- Some harms are performed without much feeling or thought, while others follow emotional arousal.
- Some harms are beneficial to the harm agent, while the benefits of others are unclear.

A theory of harm must account for these social facts. Besides, it must assimilate two other elements that I maintain characterize all harmful actions:

- Harms allow one to display desired identities.
- Harms follow the definition of the target or one's action in particular ways.

These two additional elements have to do with how we construct ourselves, including the selves we wish to be, our targets,
and our actions.

My analysis scrutinizes what we know about harm through
the lens of discourse, and specifically narrative, analysis. In this
way I hope to address the question, what is the nature of harmful action? This book offers an answer to that question through
the close examination of perpetrator accounts in four rather different cases of harm: genocide, the killing of nonhuman animals
for meat, intimate partner violence, and penal harm. The book
proceeds from an examination of differences between accounts
to an examination of what they share in common.

Chapter 2 frames the book. Here I set out key connections
between identity, narrative, and action. I also describe—in connection with harm although relatively abstractly—two logics
that inhabit our narratives: our position and our power relative
to others. Chapter 3 focuses on genocide. I analyze accounts
given by agents of the Nazi Holocaust and its leader, Adolf
Hitler, and by agents of the late twentieth-century genocide in
Rwanda, primarily involving Hutus against Tutsis. Chapter 4
considers complicity in the killing of nonhuman animals for
meat. Common themes in this case are the appeal to a sacred or
natural order juxtaposed against appeal to simple desire—or
just wanting a burger. The case of meat eating raises questions
about philosopher Charles Taylor's (1985) distinction between
strong and weak evaluation. Also germane are agents' claims to
have no or only partial knowledge of the harms they are implicated in and their desire to avoid such knowledge. Chapter 5
concerns intimate partner violence, which stands out from the
aforementioned harms in that it targets an intimate or former
intimate. Chapter 6 attends to penal harm, or the harm we do
to criminal offenders through such practices as incarceration
and execution. In Chapter 7 I synthesize the logics common
to the various harms, which are (1) the reduction of the

target, (2) harm's inevitability or the alleged propulsion by some force not under the actor's immediate control, and (3) the license to do harm. Stories that combine each of these logics conduce to harm. Chapter 8 asks, how do we eliminate or at least limit harm?

The theory offered in these pages was inspired by existing explanations of particular harms, especially crime, mass atrocities, and punishment. I began the process of developing a general theory by commingling the existing ideas with two sorts of data: interviews with individuals to learn how they legitimize harms and published accounts given by harm-complicit actors. The interviews were conducted in Tennessee with residents of the state. They were conducted one-on-one by a team of research assistants and myself and held in campus offices, libraries, coffee shops, and the homes of the research participants. The interviews were minimally structured; prompts concerned the participant's take on various harmful practices including but not limited to those examined in this book. The majority were digitally recorded and later transcribed.

A good deal of thought led me to the first set of data and the decision to interview "regular people." I have spent much of my research career interviewing known and captured criminal offenders for the purpose of discovering their perspectives on their actions and circumstances. But such specificity offers no advantage for developing a general theory of harm. By listening to those whose support for harm is ongoing I am able to clarify forward logics—those that form the basis for future harm. People express just such logics when they talk about their support of harmful practices that are either public policy or at least not illegal, where support will not get them in (much) trouble.

My goal is to clarify the relationship between the logics we convey and our harmful actions and thus to set out a narrative criminology of harm. I believe that we humans should do as little harm as we can, and that conviction motivates my quest for understanding. Clearly, the project of theorizing harm demands reflexivity from the start. Not just harmful action but also its regulation and explanation—what I am up to here—are discursive endeavors. Once we brand some action as "harm," we set in motion rhetorical processes, including academic efforts that feed public policies and practices, that may cause harm in turn. One has only to consider the case of punishment of crimes to recognize the utter seriousness of work that begins with such designations.

CHAPTER 2

We Are Written

A Narrative Framework of Harm

I AM AFTER THE CULTURAL RHETORICS that promote harm. The case studies presented in the coming chapters—concerning genocide, animal abuse, intimate partner violence, and punishment of offenders—lead me to rhetorics that communicate at their most basic level who we are. In this chapter I consider what we talk about and how we talk when we discuss ourselves and others. Two principal identity anchors or themes, position and power, are examined, along with the key role of narrative in forging identity. Whereas these are fundamentals of identity, I wed the discussion to harm, drawing connections between storied selves and harmful action.

POSITIONING THE SELF AND OTHER

Students of particular harms have paid close attention to social distance, or the extent to which we construct targets as familiar or foreign. An us-versus-them mentality is widely held to be dangerous. Supposedly, the greater the social distance between parties, the greater the likelihood of harm. Conversely, harm is inhibited when the Other is familiar. According to Emmanuel Levinas, "the face is what forbids us to kill" (1985, 86). We eat nameless chickens, not our pets. A. Ayres Boswell and Joan Spade found that the college fraternity parties that posed the

greatest rape risk for women were characterized by gender seg-
regation and that women who were strangers to the men were
most likely to be sexually assaulted: "These women are faceless
victims, nameless acquaintances—not friends. Men said that
their responsibility to such persons, and the level of guilt they
feel later if the hookups end in sexual intercourse, are much
lower if they hook up with women they do not know. In high-
risk fraternity houses, brothers treated women as subordinates
and kept them at a distance" (1996, 143). Gresham Sykes and
David Matza propose that social distance is inversely related to
the likelihood of juveniles doing harm, citing discursive stipula-
tions against harm to familiars: "'don't steal from friends' or
'don't commit vandalism against a church of your own faith'"
(1957, 665). Adolf Hitler recalls his early recognition of the
otherness of Jewish people: "Wherever I went, I began to see
Jews, and the more I saw, the more sharply they became distinguished in my eyes from the rest of humanity" ([1925] 1999,
56). Arguably, othering Jews was a prerequisite of the atrocities
against them that Hitler would later order.

Some view physical distance as interacting with social distance in the etiology of harm. Donald Black posits terrorism as
a means of addressing a grievance whose consequential features
are social and physical distance: "Terrorism arises only when a
grievance has a social geometry distant enough and a physical
geometry close enough for mass violence against civilians"
(2004, 21). For Georg Simmel, proximity highlights estrangement. In his classic essay "The Stranger," he writes, "This position of the stranger stands out more sharply if, instead of leaving
the place of his activity, he settles down there" (1971, 144).

In fact, social distance is both positively *and* negatively
related to harm. Clearly the relationship is complicated.
Whereas people do not ordinarily eat their pets, they otherwise
abuse them, as well as their partners, children, siblings, and
parents. Violence is most likely between acquaintances, not

strangers (FBI 2012). When police are able to discern the victim-offender relationship, they reveal that the majority of murder victims are known to the offender (FBI 2010). Joseph Michalski (2004) found that couples use more violence than do other pairs of individuals such as coworkers, although abuse is more likely to occur among unmarried cohabiting partners than among spouses (see also DeKeseredy 2011, 24–25). In a study by Lynn Magdol and colleagues (1998) cohabiting couples were more violent than mere daters. How to explain these contradictory findings?

Russell Jacoby suggests that our familiars pose a unique psychosocial threat: "It is not so much the unknown that threatens us but the known. We disdain and attack our brothers—our kin, our acquaintances, our neighbors—whom we know well, perhaps too well. We know their faults, their beliefs, their desires, and we distrust them *because* of that" (2011, ix–x; emphasis in original). Jacoby insists, "Like, not unlike, prompts violence" because too much similarity threatens our identities (xii). Thus, for instance, extreme Islamists "fear losing themselves by mimicking the West" (154). Another prominent example Jacoby offers is that of men terrified of the taint of the feminine. He observes that social norms separating men and women "are meant to protect men from women and from male unease at the prospect of becoming unmanned" (135). Jacoby is suggesting that violence is a remedy for too much identification with the Other, or too *little* social distance.

But women do not appear to be terrified of that which is masculine, a fact that Jacoby ignores. Identification with masculinity is no threat to them and does not lead them to do harm on any scale. It could nonetheless be said that differential socialization and social roles abridge the social distance females experience from other people or at least from their male familiars. Women might view others more universally by virtue of their early childhood experiences of identifying with mothers

(C. Gilligan 1982) and later experiences *as* mothers. This consideration of gender makes clear that social proximity and identification are achieved rather than given in any human relationship.

What about constructing others as not merely different but as bad, destructive, inferior, or subhuman? Hitler would ultimately view the Jewish people as much more than just "a foreign people" ([1925] 1999, 59): they became for him a "race of dialectical liars" (63), an "adversary of all humanity" (307), and "the eternal blood-sucker" (310). In general, characterizations of victims seem to vary with the harmful action. Mass atrocities against people run on rendering the Other as dangerous. Meat eating is facilitated by a designation of the Other as inferior. Such variety testifies to the socially contingent nature of harm worthiness.

A general cultural theory of harm demands a broader conceptualization of how we construct targets of harm. The Other is not necessarily foreign, evil, dangerous, or inferior, but in one or another instance of harm any one of these. I propose the concept of *reducing* the Other. To reduce a target is (1) to characterize the target in terms of very few interests or (2) to deny that the target has unique interests, distinguishable from others, including the perpetrator. The first gesture is highly relevant to harm to humans, including genocide, domestic violence, and penal harm. In the cases of genocide and penal harm, interests have been pared down to nefarious ones. The second gesture is most clearly seen in the context of harm to nonhumans. They are said to have "nothing going on" except those purposes we have established for them. They were made for our use.

Jody Roy observes, "Whether visual or verbal, reduction discourages us from seeing whole people" (2002, 38–39). Thus, in *Mein Kampf,* Hitler ([1925] 1999) tells a story in which "the Jew," while posing as a member of a religion, is actually a political actor who seeks to gain power time and again. That the Jew is singular for Hitler signifies a limited range of interests— not even the number of interests that multiple individuals might be expected to have. Anti-Semitism is a specific process of reduction; others are stigmatization, racism, sexism, classism, homophobia, ageism, xenophobia, and Orientalism. Reductive processes do not necessarily promote brutality, for other elements of the story, concerning one's power, matter as well.

POWER AND HARM

We construct ourselves in terms of our capacity to act; that is, in forging our identities we thematize our power or absence of power. What is the relationship between having power and doing harm? One popular argument, for which good evidence exists, is that power motivates harm doing—that it corrupts. In several experimental studies, subjects assigned to power positions came to hold more negative attitudes toward subordinates. Based on a meta-analysis of twenty-five studies, John Georgesen and Monica Harris (1998) determined that power is significantly associated with negative performance evaluations (and with positive self-evaluations). David Kipnis found that subjects assigned to a power position devalued the worth of those assigned to play their workers, expressed more manipulative attitudes about and showed less concern for their workers as individuals, desired social distance from their workers, and saw their workers as being controlled by the subject's power. Kipnis concludes that "the control of resources . . . tempts the power holder to manipulate others" ([1972] 2006, 185). Note that the objects of manipulation are not just anyone—they are persons or other beings designated as one's subordinates. If power corrupts, that corruption is nonetheless manifest in target-specific ways. A more sociological approach is warranted.

The powerful are good at escaping surveillance. They can get others to do harm for them and thereby avoid some of the censure if the harm is made public (Tittle 2004). They have the resources to post bail, hire effective lawyers, and influence legal decision makers. They also have the resources to influence the media; at the extreme, the media act as an instrument of the state. The power of state, corporate, and other group leaders partly lies in their control of knowledge about the world, including knowledge about their conduct (Berger and Luckmann 1966). Even when the powerful perpetrate harm in public, we often let them get away with it. That is, we grant the powerful permission to do harm. We allow parents to hit their children and government agents to hold people captive. These actions are acceptable *because* the harm agent wields power over the target.

Criminologists posit power as a cause of white-collar and political crime. Access and influence are generally the proposed causal mechanisms. Yet most criminologists study harm agents who are relatively powerless, marginalized on the basis of socioeconomic class, ethnicity, and the like. Conflict and critical theorists argue that crime is the behavior of the relatively powerless because criminalization is a ploy to contain them. From some theoretical perspectives, such as strain theories and feminist theories of female offending, powerlessness itself promotes offending. In short, criminological theories feature both power and powerlessness as causes of crime. Hence Charles Tittle's (1995) noteworthy reconciliation, control balance theory, explains deviance as a function of a "control surplus" *or* a "control deficit."

I propose that something about both the presence and the absence of power do indeed matter where harmful action is concerned. But my treatment of these emphasizes discursive constructions. On the one hand, we grant ourselves permission to harm because of our alleged power to do so. We entitle ourselves to harm because of our relationship with God, our place in a natural order, or some physical endowment. On the other hand, we channel a discourse of powerlessness—a logic according to which harm is necessary or inevitable and therefore the individual is incapable of preventing it. Such logics include espousals of necessity, lack of alternatives, "losing it," and not knowing about harm. Scholars and others commonly view these claims as merely ex post facto rationalizations communicated to avoid accountability. Thus, feminists are skeptical of men's declarations of powerlessness (Faludi 1999) and Holocaust scholars question the sincerity of claims by German officers during World War II that they had no choice but to comply with Nazi orders. By taking discourse seriously, we see that allegations of powerlessness may contribute to harmful action whatever their veracity. The cooperation of the license to harm and the logic of powerlessness is a *power paradox,* one of the instigators of harm discernible across case studies. How do we get away with making these contradictory claims? We weave logics of capability and compulsion together in the form of narratives.

Narrative and Action

A narrative is a type of discourse that follows events or experiences over time and makes some point (Labov and Waletzky 1967). An idea that has taken hold across academic disciplines, including anthropology, sociology, criminology, geography, philosophy, and psychology, is that social life is *narrated* or *storied*.[1] Increasingly, narrative is seen as "an ontological condition of social life" (Somers 1994, 614), as *constitutive* of reality and not merely its representation. Stories make things happen because they guide human action.

Narratives connect experiences over time—past, present, and future. Jerome Bruner calls the "inherent sequentiality" of narrative its signal characteristic (1990, 43). Hence, narrative serves as a sort of script for action, although a highly dynamic one insofar as our narratives are ever-changing. Our narratives communicate who we think we are and who we hope to be. They also connect personal experience to broader themes and norms in the culture. As Arthur Frank puts it, they "summon up whole cultures" (2010, 37). The cultural touchstones of stories are moral in nature: they pertain to right and wrong ways to act. Thus stories are devices for explaining and projecting our moral selves. Emplotted along culturally familiar trajectories of moral conduct, our experiences seem to lead us toward certain next steps and not others.

Philip Smith's work highlights the distinctive role of narrative in social action. Smith clarifies the narrative instigation of violence through case studies of Bernard Goetz's 1984 shooting of four would-be muggers on a New York City subway car and of the Persian Gulf War waged by the United States in the early 1990s. He arrives at "three stringent narrative conditions that the state and the citizen must meet to legitimize their violent acts to contemporary civil society: (1) violence must be a last resort, restrained to minimum levels, and there should be no peaceful alternatives; (2) the violence must be undertaken by a quasi-heroic 'pure' figure against an 'evil other'; and (3) the violence must be undertaken for selfless and universalistic reasons" (1997, 110). More recently Smith (2005) has presented a narrative theory of war. Here, before turning to narrative he considers the role of binary codes or discourses in structuring understandings of political conflict. These other discursive forms take him some distance in explaining nations' war making. He names the Discourse of Liberty and the Discourse of Repression as especially relevant. The Discourse of Liberty specifies open relationships regulated by rules, whereas the contrasting Discourse of Repression involves secretive and calculating relationships. He observes that "some identification of the enemy with the Discourse of Repression is a minimal requirement for war." Yet codes have their limitations:

Their exegesis and application can obfuscate or reduce complexities of meaning, flattening out the interpretive field, stamping out nuances of tone, and squeezing cultural messages into sterile boxes, thereby ignoring culture's potentials for engendering creativity, imagination, fantasy, and the projection of ethical possibility and responsibility. More importantly, an analysis of codes will not take us very far in understanding how lines of action are constructed. We might think of lots of countries as acting in ways that are consistent with the Discourse of Repression, yet we rarely declare war. Binaries help us make sense of the world but do not offer an instruction manual for what to do next. (2005, 17)

Criminologists use the concept of subcultural codes to explain conventional crime. Marvin Wolfgang and Franco Ferracuti refer to the subculture of violence as one "where physically aggressive responses are either expected or required by all members" (1967, 298). Neutralization techniques (Sykes and Matza 1957), another mainstay of criminology, are similar to codes, sanctioning transgressions with circumscribed cultural messages. Neutralization theory goes beyond subcultural theory by specifying what we tell ourselves when we tell ourselves that violence is acceptable—not altogether but given present circumstances. One might neutralize and subsequently proceed with some problematic deed by denying responsibility, which lets the actor off the moral hook. Or one might appeal to higher loyalties, reasoning that the deed serves a purpose more important than the norm that says refrain from misconduct.

The idea that we sanction our norm violations with codes (violation is good or acceptable) or neutralizations (*this* violation is good or acceptable) is reasonable enough, but I agree with Philip Smith that narratives give us a better handle on harmful action. Like discourses, codes and neutralizations suggest very little about the character, aspirations, and passions of the actor. The concept of narrative permits a richer account of social actors, highlighting both creativity and structure—bringing into view more of those cultural messages that move them. And move them they do: actors go overboard because of incitement by stories. They do not simply fulfill directives. Arthur Frank enumerates the capacities of stories, including the capacity to excite. Stories can "make one particular perspective not only plausible but compelling" (2010, 31) and "make life dramatic and remind people that endings are never assured" (32). They "inform people's sense of what counts as good and bad, of how to act and how not to act" (36). Because they give recollected experience a universal and thus a transcendent quality, they tend to arouse our emotions more than other forms of discourse, such as metaphors and reports. Stories capture our imaginations in a way that other discursive forms simply do not.

In addition to their unique potential to animate, stories and narratives allow us to deploy contradictory codes and neutralizations. For instance, an actor might both deny responsibility for a harmful action and deny that it causes injury: "I can't help it. Anyway, it won't hurt anyone." To speak that way could make the speaker seem incoherent—something sounds fishy—since one need not justify behavior for which one is allegedly not responsible. Narratives help us to achieve coherence, or at least the appearance of coherence (Sandberg 2013). As Francesca Polletta observes, "we find a story coherent because it resonates with stories we have heard before" (2006, 10). A familiar story can merge contradictory claims, if not seamlessly then at least in a way that is culturally plausible. I want to tweak that observation: a familiar story can also make certain inconsistencies acceptable.

An example of incoherence conveyed as common logic through stories involves J. David Adkisson, who in 2008 perpetrated a mass shooting at a Unitarian church in Knoxville, Tennessee, that killed two and wounded six others. Adkisson relayed his life story in a letter written prior to the shooting and with me in subsequent research interviews in prison (Presser 2012). Using the story form and drawing on metaphors signaling, among other things, the rightful place of self vis-à-vis Other, Adkisson was able to construct a ruined protagonist who finally defeats his antagonists with one heroic deed. Identifying congregants as liberals, Adkisson took it upon himself to represent "decent honest Americans [who] can't fight this liberalism through the ballot box." He emphasized agency in calling the shooting "an act of political protest" but also referred to his helplessness, lamenting that his troubled life "came to that." Thus was his violence both strategically deployed and compelled. I argue that such inconsistency is a key engine of harm.

Toward a Narrative Criminology

In the chapters that follow I probe position, power, powerlessness, and related themes as they appear in verbalizations pertaining to specific harms. The study across chapters aligns with narrative criminology, where the main explanatory variable is one's story. Narrative criminology is inquiry based on a view of stories as inspiring, sustaining, or curbing harmful action. Examples from criminology are Shadd Maruna's (2001) analysis of the desistance narratives of former property offenders and Sveinung Sandberg's (2013) case study of one terrorist's "manifesto." Outside of the discipline, myriad accounts of harm emphasize narratives (see, e.g., Kay 2005; Mason 2002; P. Smith 1997, 2005; Sternberg 2003; Vetlesen 2005). Stories in these works are shown to have spurred the actions of the communicating agent. Likewise, narrative criminology takes a constitutive, as opposed to representative, view of stories: they are seen as constructing lived experience as much as lived experience constructs them (Presser 2009; Sandberg 2010).

Narrative bears some likeness to more established constructs in criminology and sociology: neutralization, cognitive error, identity, and situational interpretation. As previously discussed, neutralizations in particular are similar to narratives of harm in discursively legitimizing untoward conduct. However, neutralizations are cruder devices that, as currently conceived, fail to arouse the emotions as narratives can. In addition, scholars have sited all those constructs at the individual level, in bodies and minds, whereas narratives are formed and exist in the collective space of language. As such, narratives are readily available for scrutiny, unlike, say, cognitions and interpretations, which are always a matter of speculation, even to their possessors (cf. Jenkins 2008). I consider those other constructs as possible elements of the stories that we tell ourselves about ourselves before we do harm. The next four chapters investigate different sorts of actions for stories and story elements. My analyses of harm to bodies and spirits stand at a remove from structural forces that precede the harm. In so doing, I hope to gain and privilege a view of the ways in which such forces are captured in words.

CHAPTER 3

Genocide, Harm of Harms

EACH YEAR ON THE CAMPUS of the University
of Tennessee, Knoxville, in a grassy area between the
Humanities and Social Sciences building and the main library,
activists against abortion mount an outdoor installation of
large vivid photos allegedly depicting fetuses removed from
women's wombs. Signs leading up to the installation read
"Warning: Genocide Pictures Ahead." Several of my colleagues
have taken issue with the activists' equating abortion with
genocide. They reason that genocide—the purposive elimination of a people—is nothing like abortion, the purposive
elimination of a fetus.[1] I suspect that the activists, not much
concerned with accuracy, want to designate abortion as the
worst kind of harm imaginable, and that harm is genocide.
Genocide has been called "the crime of crimes" (Schabas 2000).
It strikes us as the worst possible harm because its eliminationist
intent is absolute and explicit, because large numbers of
people are harmed or meant to be harmed, and because it is
often associated with unthinkable atrocities. And so I begin my
exposition of a theory of harm with the worst possible harm,
genocide, of which history regrettably offers many examples.
I limit my empirical reference points to two twentieth-century
genocides—that of Nazi Germany (1933–1945) and that of
Rwanda (1994), the first being the paradigmatic genocide of
living memory, the second infamous for its face-to-face brutality. Whereas this book highlights the role of discourse and

specifically stories in all harm, that role is especially vivid in the case of genocide.

THE GENOCIDAL TARGET

First, we should entertain how genocide perpetrators represent their victims. Victims and would-be victims are central to only a few theories of crime. They are fragmented communities in social disorganization theory (Sampson, Raudenbush, and Earls 1997). Residents of such communities lack "collective efficacy," which theorists use to explain their communities' higher crime rates. Crime victims are attractive, unguarded targets in routine activities theory (Cohen and Felson 1979). According to that theory, the place, object, or person that is unprotected, accessible, and desirable to the motivated offender is at relatively high risk of being victimized.

The aforementioned observations reflect realist conceptions of factors that affect victimization risk.[2] On the matter of how offenders construct victims—what victims are made to signify— only one criminological approach is explicitly attentive: Gresham Sykes and David Matza's (1957) neutralization theory. Targets of delinquent action figure into denial of injury and denial of victim, two of the five "techniques of neutralization" that Sykes and Matza identify. It makes sense that neutralization theory, rooted as it is in social constructionism, has been applied to genocide (Alvarez 1997) because the true characteristics and conduct of genocide's victims are irrelevant to genocide. The target as conjured is what matters. Daniel Jonah Goldhagen makes this argument, providing as evidence the surreal and flexible nature of constructions of the Jews in Europe, even in those historical periods and sites when and where actual contact with Jews was lacking. Various types of anti-Semitism are seen throughout history, characterizing Jews in different ways. Anti-Semitism becomes genocidal only when Jews are constructed as "beings whose very existence constitutes a violation of the moral fabric of society" (1996, 38). During the Nazi period, "the Jew, der Jude, was both a metaphysical and an existential threat, as real to Germans as that of a powerful enemy army poised on Germany's borders for the attack" (88). The threat of the Jews was not well founded, but that fact did not prevent the harm.

In the previous chapter I explored whether social distance, or constructing the Other as different, promotes harm. I concluded that social distance bears no straightforward relation to harmful action, but reduction of the Other does. The concept of reduction stretches to accommodate reduction to threat and reduction to nonhuman. The latter warrants particular attention, given how regularly it appears in the genocide literature.

Dehumanization

If we are to render the Other as distinct, it seems that we can do so no more effectively than by casting them out of the species. Culturally, despite evidence of certain strong cross-species similarities, species is treated as an essential boundary—a marker of radical difference. Jody Roy offers, "When we dehumanize another person, we strip 'them' of any connection they might possibly have to 'us'" (2002, 17).

Dehumanization appears prominently in discussions of mass harm.[3] Herbert Kelman observes, "Dehumanization of the enemy is a common phenomenon in any war situation. Sanctioned massacres, however, presuppose a degree of dehumanization that is considerably more extreme." By dehumanization Kelman means exclusion from the "human family" and the recognition of individuality and concern that that expression implies. He continues, "Thus when a group of people is defined entirely in terms of a category to which they belong, and when this category is excluded from the human family, then the moral restraints against killing them are more readily overcome" (1973, 49). Other scholars likewise use dehumanization to signify exclusion

from the moral community of which the speaker is a part (e.g.,
Alvarez 1997; Bélanger-Vincent 2009; Fox and Levin 1998;
Huggins, Haritos-Fatouros, and Zimbardo 2002). But I would
argue that dehumanization is a problematic concept, both
empirically and ideologically. First, harm agents do not consistently construct their victims as nonhumans. Second, use of
the term takes for granted that to be nonhuman is to warrant
maltreatment.

When dehumanizing rhetoric is actually scrutinized as
verbalization, it is seen to be selective. Violators compare their
enemies to *particular* nonhumans. Adalbert, a Rwandan killer
interviewed by journalist Jean Hatzfeld (2003, 132), makes this
point explicitly: "When we spotted a small group of runaways
trying to escape by creeping through the mud, we called them
snakes. Before the killings, we usually called them cockroaches.
But during, it was more suitable to call them snakes, because of
their attitude, or zeros, or dogs, because in our country we
don't like dogs; in any case, they were less-than-nothings."[4]
Notwithstanding Adalbert's remarks, victims of the 1994
Rwanda genocide were most often labeled as cockroaches, or
inyenzi. In any case, the victims in Rwanda were clearly constructed not as just any nonhuman, but only as those considered
despicable. Cockroaches and dogs, not cows, in Rwanda; rats,
not rabbits, in Germany. Being despicable, not being nonhuman, seems to matter. Not only were the Tutsis reduced to
nonhumans: they were also "less-than-nothings" (Hatzfeld
2003, 152) and "pathetic little nobodies" (Mukanyiligira 1999,
10). Nor are all of those dehumanized targeted for genocide.
Daniel Jonah Goldhagen observes that "Germans treated other
peoples whom the Nazis and most Germans deemed to be
inferior, even 'subhuman,' such as Poles, far differently and
better than Jews" (1996, 116). Insulting the bourgeoisie,
Adolf Hitler compared them to wolves, although he did not
seek to eliminate them per se ([1925] 1999, 464). What is more,

Hitler used the same animal reference to praise his loyal storm troopers (505).[5]

Hitler and his Nazi followers used animal terms for Jews, but they also ascribed to them a variety of human characteristics. Hitler attributes "infinite shrewdness" ([1925] 1999, 319) to Jews, whose "great men are only great in the destruction of humanity and its culture" (352). The Jew has "the sure eye of the prophet" and "like a wizard" he devises his immoral conquests (382). He sees the Jew "diverting public attention from himself and occupying it elsewhere" (560), always with "amazing adroitness" (626). These are *super*human, not subhuman, characterizations. Evidently, dehumanization is not foundational to genocide.

Furthermore, the leap from nonhuman animal to target of harm is not generally theorized; it is taken for granted. Maureen Hiebert observes that dehumanization "is not the motivation for genocide, as much of the existing genocide literature suggests, but, instead, provides an understanding of the victim group that is necessary in order for the actual extermination to take place. . . . Victims of genocide are nonetheless dehumanized by being equated with 'animals,' 'vermin,' or 'pests' so that the actual act of exterminating whole groups of people becomes intellectually comprehensible and psychologically tolerable." Hiebert notes that dehumanization is "not enough to lead to genocide, because to see members of a particular group as subhuman is not to impute to them the capacity or the power to constitute an overwhelming moral threat" (2008, 13). Even as Hiebert qualifies the role of this form of reduction, she, like Herbert Kelman (1973), who inspires her analysis, does not question the fact that nonhuman equates to morally irrelevant.

Paulo Freire's use of "dehumanization" codifies it as denying the Other's freedom or capacity to act, rather than characterizing the Other as a different species of being. Humanization "is thwarted by injustice, exploitation, oppression, and the violence of the oppressors; it is affirmed by the yearning of the oppressed for freedom and justice, and by their struggle to recover their lost humanity" (1970, 28). This way of constructing the target gets us closer to the fact that violators fundamentally reduce their targets.

REDUCING THE TARGET

My conceptualization of reduction emphasizes interests. The harm agent identifies the interests of the target very narrowly. Compared with Othering and dehumanization, the reduction of targets, more broadly applicable across harms, is a more accurate description of the denigrating process that promotes genocidal harm.

In the case of genocide, whatever else targets are reduced to, they are always reduced to evil. They are *essentially* enemies. One Rwandan government official proclaimed, "Every person has a right to life, except the enemy, for the simple reason that he is the enemy" (Icyitegetse 2000, 7). The Jews are ever and fundamentally Germany's adversary in Adolf Hitler's construction. The pursuit of world domination is an "endeavor [that] lies profoundly rooted in their essential nature" ([1925] 1999, 661). Those are the rhetorics of genocide instigators—leaders. Their hateful rhetoric is commonly called propaganda, which appears to be a prerequisite to genocide (Day and Vandiver 2000). Christopher Browning suggests that genocide's foot soldiers may hold more nuanced views: "It would seem that even if the men of Reserve Police Battalion 101 had not consciously adopted the anti-Semitic doctrines of the regime, they had at least accepted the assimilation of the Jews into the image of the enemy" (1993, 73). But Daniel Jonah Goldhagen disputes the notion that German citizens did not abide by the same virulent form of anti-Semitism as the Holocaust's engineers and propagandists. Rather, he points to "eliminationist anti-semitism" as "the regnant cultural cognitive model of Jews" across Germany's Christian citizens and historical periods for centuries (1996, 115).

In Rwanda it was government officials who used more measured language when discussing the enemy than did many of the citizens interviewed by journalists for Radio Rwanda. Leaders insisted on the violence as war and expressed a wish for peace, as when Prime Minister Jean Kambanda made these remarks on May 1, 1994: "The RPF [Rwandan Patriotic Front] kills everything in its way. We are therefore asking it to end these killings so that hostilities can come to an end" (1994, 8). Citizens' messages were more bloodthirsty: "We shall swallow them whole" (Mukanyiligira 1999, 6). A Hutu citizen expressed a commitment to violence in this way: "My advice to the *Inyenzi* is that they should cease [combat], because we are not prepared to negotiate with them" (14). It is safe to say that frontline perpetrators of genocidal harm reduce their victims with rhetoric that is some version or another of their leaders'. For both the target is made to mean danger.

License to Slaughter: Reasons and Retribution

In general, a license to harm is a tangible or intangible positive referent that authorizes one's harmful actions. It is a principle, norm, rule, edict, or piece of legislation. Basic examples are "It's the law," "It's God's will," "It's my duty," "It's my right," and "It's only right." Each of these verbalizations foregrounds the *power* available to the actor—direct or indirect, provisional or permanent. Although a more wide-ranging concept, the license to harm is comparable to Gresham Sykes and David Matza's neutralization technique of appealing to higher loyalties. Sykes and Matza had in mind normative loyalty to "smaller social groups" (1957, 669), whereas the license to harm may involve loyalty to any social group, position, order, or precept, including those of the mainstream.

Adolf Hitler refers repeatedly to religious and moral license to harm in his tome *Mein Kampf*. He pronounces, "Hence today I believe that I am acting in accordance with the will of the Almighty Creator: *by defending myself against the Jew, I am fighting for the work of the Lord*" ([1925] 1999, 65; emphasis in original); it is a "sacred duty" (640). He maintains that "the right to apply even the most brutal weapons" follows from high aims and ideals (533). Likewise, the interim president of Rwanda during the 1994 genocide, Théodore Sindikubwabo, pronounced, "it is our collective duty to wage and win this war" (Kantengwa 1999, 18).

A license typical of genocide concerns retribution. A story of past injustice at the hands of the targets is told; the genocide is collective punishment (Hagan and Rymond-Richmond 2009). Rwandan Hutus repeatedly spoke of *inyenzi* paying for their treasonous acts with their lives (Mukanyiligira 1999). The injustice wrought by the targets may be more or less real, more or less fabricated. The important point is that the retributive principle authorizes the present violence. That principle may be an unspoken motif, but it lends legitimacy to a narrative: A therefore B. The license to harm largely originates with the engineers of genocide and not with its foot soldiers. Leaders are duty bound to give reasons why the genocidal project is right. Having set out such reasons, others are influenced by them—though not solely by them.

CLAIMS OF POWERLESSNESS

Harm perpetrators also claim to lack the power *not* to perpetrate the harms they do. Whereas the license to harm permits harmful action, the claim to powerlessness compels it. Actors *must* act this way: harm, either the entire project or their participation in it, is mandatory, unstoppable, inevitable.

Jack Katz prefaces his analysis of violence with the observation that a "sense of being determined by the environment, of being pushed away from one line of action and pulled toward another, is natural to everyday, routine human experience" (1988, 4). Katz's stance is uncommon. Harm doers' claims to being pushed or pulled in the direction of their misdeeds are rarely taken at face value. After all, harm is the use of power. René Girard states, "Men can dispose of their violence more efficiently if they regard the process not as something emanating from within themselves, but as a necessity imposed from without, a divine decree whose least infraction calls down terrible punishment" (1977, 14). From this perspective, a wish to avoid blame, including self-blame, motivates the rhetoric of powerlessness. Other scholars draw a connection between doing harm and seizing power. For Hannah Arendt, people act violently because their power is at risk: "Power and violence are opposites; where the one rules absolutely, the other is absent. Violence appears where power is in jeopardy, but left to its own course it ends in power's disappearance" (1969, 56). Violence thus serves the pursuit of power, and a lack of power is quite compatible with violence.

But I want to argue something that deemphasizes lack of power as a "real" thing in the world. Claims of powerlessness, even among the evidently powerful, are themselves animating logics. The claims are various. Genocide perpetrators in Germany and Rwanda stated that they or their deputies or collaborators were overcome by emotion, overtaken by the body, or simply doing "what was done." They were yielding to an atmosphere that demanded harm; they were following orders; or they were compelled to avoid loss or realize gain.

Frustration and Emotion

In a May 24, 1994, Radio Rwanda broadcast, minister of health Dr. Casimir Bizimungu expressed regret for what could not be stopped in the days following the assassination of President Juvénal Habyarimana:

> Eh well, after assassinating the President, there was a . . . the masses were furious, the population flew into a fury eh . . . which made that, what I personally did not wish and I would not witness the carnage that we saw, but the fury of the masses was such that eh . . . there have been certainly eh . . . massacres. (Radio Rwanda 1994, 28)

We cannot verify the truth of the people's fury or its overwhelming character. Criminologists have offered theories according to which strong emotion is a prerequisite to violence (e.g., Agnew 1992; Dollard et al. 1939). In stark contrast is Hannah Arendt's (1963) view of "the banality of evil," as seen by heartless and routine engagement in Nazi atrocities. Against both perspectives, I offer *stories* of unstoppable emotion as a factor in harm. Actors are not necessarily driven to violence by rage, but they enact tales of such.

GROUP DEFENSE

Threat is the primary ideological impetus to genocide. Targets may pose physical or cultural danger: genocide extinguishes that danger. Philosopher Arne Johan Vetlesen observes, "In all cases of genocide in the twentieth century, the action taken by one's own group typically assumes the character of *self-defence*" (2005, 150; emphasis in original). Adolf Hitler maintained that Germany must seize land to "free it from the danger of vanishing from the earth or of serving others as a slave nation" ([1925] 1999, 646). A Radio Rwanda journalist reflected on the need for listeners to "defend [Rwanda's] territorial integrity, to prevent the enemy from wrecking [sic] havoc in our country" (Mukanyiligira 1999, 24). One might ask what distinguishes a discourse of defense, conjuring a self at risk, from a discourse of retribution, conjuring a self licensed to harm.

To state the difference most simply, the rhetoric of self-defense anticipates a future threat, whereas the rhetoric of injustice recalls a past wrong. The former suggests a protagonist whose "back is to the wall." Necessity in this case governs action.

THE WILL OF THE BODY

If protecting the physical and national body is a fundamental discourse of genocide, the body also acts of its own accord, beyond individual will. Perpetrators of genocide appeal to what their bodies dictate. The physicality of the genocidal project envelopes the actor. It is usually frontline perpetrators rather than planners who appeal to the body's will. A Rwandan killer named Joseph-Désiré recounted the unwilled experience of genocide:

> The one who rushed off machete in hand, he listened to nothing anymore. He forgot everything, first of all his level of intelligence. Doing the same thing every day meant we didn't have to think about what we were doing. We went out and came back without having a single thought. We hunted because it was the order of the day, until the day was over. Our arms ruled our heads; in any case our heads no longer had their say. (Hatzfeld 2003, 50)

Joseph-Désiré here conveys just how corporeal and mindless the killing was for him and others.

For some of the new cultural criminologists, individuals engage in risky activities known as edgework to resolve issues of control, with the body at the center of that dramatic resolution. One seeks to wrest control over one's body from "rational" social orders (Presdee 2000) or to make transcendent meaning out of one's "own inner contingency" (Lyng 2004, 369). Social processes stop. Chaos beckons, leading the body to let loose. In contrast, in my account bodies letting loose and chaos beckoning are story elements.

THE ATMOSPHERE

More often than the rule of the body, perpetrators of genocide evoke the rule of the atmosphere. The situation simply compels. Elie, another Rwandan genocidaire interviewed by Jean Hatzfeld, shared that "the job pulled us along" (2003, 120). Summarizing these and similar remarks, Hatzfeld notes that speakers "assert that they were carried away in a tumult, an uproar, a commotion—words they often use" (215). Theories of the compulsion of the social setting—it is clearly a *social* setting that compels—include those of Gustav Le Bon and David Matza.

For Le Bon "the crowd" eliminates the possibility of individual reasoning: "The fact that [individuals] have been transformed into a crowd puts them in possession of a sort of collective mind which makes them feel, think, and act in a manner quite different from that in which each individual of them would feel, think, and act were he in a state of isolation" (1903, 19). Le Bon proposes that the collective mind takes over by three means: a "sentiment of invincible power," contagion, and suggestibility (22). Whereas individuals usually bring logic and evidence to bear on claims they hear and make, a "crowd scarcely distinguishes between the subjective and the objective" (33). Le Bon notes that people in a crowd are especially prone to being persuaded by discourses that they would critically evaluate as individuals: "The improbable does not exist for a crowd, and it is necessary to bear this circumstance well in mind to understand the facility with which are created and propagated the most improbable legends and stories" (32). Joseph-Désiré supports Le Bon's conceptualization in recounting what participation in the Rwandan genocide was like: "It became a madness that went on all by itself. You raced ahead or you got out of the way to escape being run over, but you followed the crowd" (Hatzfeld 2003, 50). Whereas Le Bon *describes* the collective mind, Matza (1964) *explains* it—why a person's volition seems irrelevant in certain social settings. Matza clarifies a process that individuals engage in when they associate with others.

Before choosing to perpetrate a delinquent act, the youth—Matza's main subject—experiences what Matza calls a mood of fatalism. A sense of injustice and a subcultural belief in destiny engender the mood of fatalism. Where do these come from? Matza (1964) observes that juveniles co-opt the logics of the mainstream, even as they distort them (see also Matza and Sykes 1961; Sykes and Matza 1957). A belief in human powerlessness—of oneself "as an effect"—is conventional in most cultures, as is the opposite idea, that human beings are agents or "causes" (88). Neutralizations, such as denial of responsibility and appeal to higher loyalties, are societal vehicles for such ideas.

According to Matza, the company of peers also drives the mood of fatalism: "Once the concept of destiny is enlarged, the situation of company may remind the delinquent of himself as effect. He is one of many. He is in a state of acute dependency, especially if he has been thrust into the hands of the company by a prior incident; but the company itself may also elicit the mood of fatalism since it too 'pushes around' many of its members" (1964, 90). In turn, the mood of fatalism might put the individual in a state of drift, or "episodic release from moral constraint" (69). The mood of fatalism spurs a desire to take control:

It is likely to culminate in a sense of desperation among persons who place profound stress on the capacity to control the surroundings. . . . Naturally enough, they seek to undo or cast away so unpleasant and undesired a state of being. They seek, in other words, to restore the mood of humanism in which the self is experienced as cause—the state in which man himself makes things happen. . . . The restoration of the humanistic mood—and incidentally the restoration of the moral bind that is implicit in the

responsible character of the humanistic mood—may be
accomplished by the commission of infraction. (189;
emphasis in original)

Arne Johan Vetlesen's theory of collective violence runs on
logic parallel to Matza's theory of juvenile delinquency, with
individuals experiencing their will as dwarfed by that of the
group:

> Suppressing and bracketing *individual* agency when per-
> forming *collective* evil is both a crucial psychological pre-
> condition and a "lived" consequence of such evildoing,
> operative in both respects to the extent that the acting
> individual starts behaving *as though* he is not responsible for
> what he does, having internalized the ideological notion
> that the individual's agency-based freedom counts for
> nothing, and his or her collective identity-cum-destiny for
> everything, whereby (collective) evil is made out to be
> imperative and necessary, not optional and avoidable.
> (2005, 146–147; emphasis in original)

For both Matza and Vetlesen, the individual acts on conventional logics about power and powerlessness, agency and destiny.

Vetlesen's assailants "suppress" and "bracket" their agency,
but such moves are not necessarily deliberate. Indeed, Matza's
emphasis on mood counters the view of behavior as considered.
Daniel Silver observes that "being in a mood" or "the felt sense
of being called upon to respond to a situation" (2011, 210) is
common: the "experience of being drawn upon and solicited is
more fundamental than that of choosing and willing; in fact . . .
effort is a derivative rather than basic dimension of action"
(200). Silver continues, "A theory of the moodiness of action . . .
permits clear formulations about variations in the conditions
under which situations may or may not be experienced in their
compelling character" (214), yet he leaves for another day just

what conditions the moodiness of certain settings. Rhetorics that hinge on identities—who we are—do the job; these put us "in a mood." Our behavior takes place within an environment of communicated signals, many of which go unnoticed—akin to behavioral psychology's discriminative stimuli. That reactions to communicated signals seem to be instantaneous does not preclude their discursive basis.

Following Orders

Front-line agents of mass harm commonly speak of being bound to orders. Ishmael Beah, a child soldier in Sierra Leone, recalls the moment before killing a prisoner: "I didn't feel a thing for him, didn't think that much about what I was doing. I just waited for the corporal's order" (2007, 124). The argument that one was merely following orders is frequently met with cynicism. A common response is that one actually had more power than that claim implies. Thus, Christopher Browning seeks to prove the error of claims of irrefutable directives during the reign of the Third Reich. In *Ordinary Men,* his careful account of Reserve Battalion 101, a unit of the German Order Police that participated in the killing of thousands of Jews from 1941 to 1943, he demonstrates that the officers did not really *have to* follow orders to kill: "each individual policeman once again had a considerable degree of choice" (1993, 127). He could opt out; sanctions for doing so were not great. "Quite simply, in the past forty-five years no defense attorney or defendant in any of the hundreds of postwar trials has been able to document a single case in which refusal to obey an order to kill unarmed civilians resulted in the allegedly inevitable dire punishment" (170). Browning considers whether the officers *anticipated* punishment, whatever its actual eventuality. His research leads him to conclude that the men knew in advance they could avoid shooting, so "a situation of positive duress did not exist in the battalion" (171).

I maintain that a rhetoric of following orders facilitated Nazi atrocities regardless of the veracity of that rhetoric. Browning's own discussion of what he believes caused the killings helps to illuminate that effect: "Those who did not shoot risked isolation, rejection, and ostracism—a very uncomfortable prospect within the framework of a tight-knit unit stationed abroad among a hostile population, so that the individual had virtually nowhere else to turn for support and social contact" (1993, 185). With its putative orders, the hierarchy offered a vocabulary of reasons to perpetrate harm, allowing morally ambivalent killers to avoid calling forth the very isolation they feared, had they reasoned *in its terms*.

Individual allegiance to some code may not reflect true commitment to it (Anderson 1999; Matza 1964). The need to appear as a team player can lead the individual to articulate the party line as to what forces one's hand—in the case of genocide it is sanctions meted out by higher-ups. The individual is not disingenuous in articulating those reasons, or at least not necessarily. The way we talk about the parameters for our conduct has a life of its own. In situ, speakers infrequently contemplate the truth-value of those parameters-as-spoken. I used to tell students that I "cannot" give them the grade they wanted instead of the one they received. This was untrue—I did have that capacity—and yet I was never aware of deceiving anyone by using that common expression of incapacity. Nor are perpetrators of genocidal violence necessarily intent on deceiving themselves or others by asserting limited agency. These may be excuses, but that is by no means all that they are.

THE LURE OF GAIN AND THE THREAT OF LOSS

A final logic of powerlessness is the exigency of achieving gain and avoiding loss. The "need" to move ahead in some material way or to resist falling behind, in the context of genocide, is constructed in urgent terms. Both were clearly expressed in the Rwandan context. Jean-Baptiste, whom Jean Hatzfeld interviewed, reported that the desire for pecuniary gain overwhelmed his and his peers' agency: "The more we killed, the more greediness urged us on" (2003, 49) and "We could no longer stop ourselves from wielding the machete, it brought us so much profit" (87).

No doubt, theft of money, land, houses, animals, art, and so forth frequently accompanies genocidal violence. Rational choice theorists would argue that the promise of such booty animates genocide; it might at least inspire passivity in the face of genocide. But the overboard character of much violence and especially mass violence weighs against rational choice explanations. Consider perpetrators of genocide going beyond killing their victims, denigrating the body, seemingly enthralled by their own perversity, such as pertains to "the white people whose legs and arms we shall amputate, so that they will return to Belgium without arms" (Mukanyiligira 1999, 20) and intoxicated German officers "shooting the remaining Jews 'for sport'" (Browning 1993, 134). It is hard to fathom the rewards of such excesses or their estimation by actors in advance. I propose that *depicting* those rewards as irresistible and one's self as under their spell is part of the motivational structure of genocidal action.

THE WHOLE STORY:
A POWER PARADOX

Logics of license and powerlessness regularly come together in broad statements justifying mass harm. Anthropologist Ariane Bélanger-Vincent (2009) observes, "In the War on Terrorism context, self-defense is united with the U.S. executive branch's constitutional authority to protect the country" (2009, 41). Adolf Hitler asserted that given "the complete subjection of the present state to Marxism . . . the National Socialist movement really acquires the duty, not only of preparing the victory of its idea, but of taking over its defense against the terror of an International drunk with victory" ([1925] 1999, 535). Similarly, Hitler proclaimed "the right to possess soil can become a duty if without extension of its soil a great nation seems doomed to destruction" ([1925] 1999, 654). "I have the *right* to do it; I *have* to do it." I call the coincidence of such discourses a power paradox. The two assertions would seem to contradict each other. But they form a unit, one that I suggest promotes harm.

The tension between freedom and constraint is a universal aspect of human experience. In stories animating genocide the tension is amplified. First, in such stories, freedom and constraint pertain to epic values and experiences—one's survival and the survival of family, community, and homeland; one's god and all that that god ordains. Second, these are talked about using the most dramatic idioms available—"There's no time to falter! The future is in your hands!"—thereby creating a heady blend of personifications of the self and of those who would stand in the way of the realization of that self. The combination is captivating: How should one act? How *can* one? It stands to arouse a desire to break out violently and simultaneously provides reasons why it is all right to do so. The word "right" is crucial in this context. It signifies both that something is allowed and that something is just. The cry of justice, however one defines it, tends to grip us.

Whereas the power paradox sounds amiss when presented as two adjacent statements, it is not generally articulated that way. Rather, the power paradox is conveyed in stories. We are in the middle of our stories, working out the rest based on how we represent what has come before. If we represent events and circumstances so far in the dizzying terms of the power paradox, we may well write murderous action by the heroic protagonist into the story.

Stories of genocide tend to be apocalyptic, the message being that when "radical evil is afoot in the world there can be no compromise, no negotiated solution, no prudent efforts to effect sanctions or to maintain a balance of power" (Smith 2005, 27). The people behind the genocides in Germany and in Rwanda, leaders and everyone else, conjured radical evil embodied in a reduced antagonist. Their vivid tales contained the seeds of the power paradox I have described, emphasizing both fate—bending one's will—and fault—demanding reprisal.

CHAPTER 4

Institutionalized Harm
through Meat Eating

UNLIKE GENOCIDE, WHICH FIGURES promi-
nently in the public imagination as harm, most of us take for
granted the killing of nonhuman animals for food. The killing of
nonhumans is mundane and implicates most of us. How do we
do it? One answer is that we do not. In these times, for large
segments of the world's population, we delegate the killing of
animals to other agents and reenter the scene as consumers of
meat. I am referring here to the multibillion-dollar factory farm
and meatpacking industries. These industries see to it that the
harm they do to animals is largely invisible, in part by dissemi-
nating mystifying vocabularies. Activists have succeeded in
exposing harm to nonhumans, although people selectively take
up the available information.

This chapter probes the logics of harm to nonhumans from
meat eating, a case of highly institutionalized harm. The chapter
is built on qualitative interviews with sixty meat eaters as well as
scholarly and popular works concerning meat eating.[1] As with
genocide, speakers reduced their targets—here quite radically,
to objects. They claimed a license to harm and emphasized their
powerlessness not to harm or to stop harm. They drew on an
array of cultural themes to make these claims, having to do,
for example, with custom, habit, and evolutionary adaptation.
Few of those we interviewed offered reasons for meat eating

embedded in stories, which I attribute to the fact that meat eating is habitual and normative, qualities that do not generally incite storytelling.

REDUCTION OF NONHUMANS

We saw in chapter 3 that genocidal agents conjure a threatening Other. In contrast, those implicated in the killing of animals for meat conjure them as mostly benign: they reduce them to objects for human use. The objectification of nonhumans could be quite literal, as when research participant Brie called farm animals "things that are actually raised for slaughter."[2] And Ali reasoned, "I figure it's their purpose in life to be eaten," thus implying that nonhumans do not have interests independent of humans. Speakers conveyed a good deal of awareness about the role that reduction plays in their ability to eat meat. Several told us that they could not eat the flesh of an animal they had known. Ann observed, "When you look at the meat section, you're looking for a good-looking steak. . . . You don't think of the cow itself." Similarly, Michelle explained, "I'll go to the store and buy [meat] 'cause I don't know that cow, but I wouldn't eat the cow that I knew the name to." These speakers emphasized the role of language ("steak") or its absence—the absence of a name for the animal—in the reduction of nonhumans.

Institutional Logics

The reduction of nonhuman animals is big business. From birth to death, on farms and in so-called processing plants and slaughterhouses, animals including chickens, turkeys, pigs, cows, fish, and shellfish are conceived as "mere pieces of biological equipment used for the manufacture of protein" (Hamilton 2006, 158). The terms "meat" and "seafood" denote animal flesh rendered suitable as food—a reduced form of matter. Animals are resources, counted, for example, in pounds and not as individuals; their suffering is hidden behind terms usually reserved for objects, like "bird *damage*" instead of injury (Stibbe 2001, 155). The vitality of nonhumans is denied both before and after they are killed (Adams 1994).

Meat eaters deploy similar language. Not surprisingly, all of our research participants used terms that signify reduced non-humans: meat, pork, bacon, steak, poultry, and so forth. This is common parlance. Besides, several spoke as though living animals are already their dead selves—already the food they would be made into. Ann shared, "When I see a cow, I think, 'Oh, that could go in my freezer.'" Don referred to animals as food in the following exchange:

INTERVIEWER: Do you eat meat?
DON: Yes.
INTERVIEWER: Okay. I do too, so that's not a judgment call.
DON: [*Light chuckle.*]
INTERVIEWER: But, um. Is that harm?
DON: No. That's food.
INTERVIEWER: No, that's food.
DON: That's food.
INTERVIEWER: Uh. [*Pause.*] It's okay to kill them because . . .
DON: It's okay to kill animals . . . because they're . . . food. That's what they're for.
INTERVIEWER: That's what they're for. [Pause.] Is that harming them?
DON: Not if it's done in a humane way.

Don declined to assign nonhumans victim status. As Donileen Loseke explains in outlining the constructionist approach to social problems, "any particular person is not a victim or a villain until someone classifies the person in that way" (2003, 14). Loseke herself excludes the possibility that victims (or villains) may be non-persons. Our research participants are doing and saying nothing that is not done and said by those who spend much of their time thinking about harm, not to mention those who plan that harm.

What Is Not Said

We promote harm by failing to introduce into discussion certain harms and harm targets; Judith Butler calls this "a refusal of discourse" (2004, 36). Actually, discourse exclusion characterizes all speech. We say what we say by *not* saying countless other things. That this is the rule does not mean that it is neutral activity.

Nonhumans are left out of all sorts of ethical discussions. For example, they are rarely considered victims of crime. Piers Beirne observes, "Animals' role as the property of humans tends to be their master status in criminology" (2009, 3). When criminal law has dealt with nonhumans, it has mainly dealt with them as stolen objects—just as prohibitions against rape have historically had to do with theft of male property. When attention truly turns to animals as victims, what gets examined are the rather unusual activities of individuals and not the mass harm enterprises in which most of us are implicated.

As discussed in previous chapters, scholars call the exclusion from compassionate consideration and disempowerment, leading to the victimization of humans, *dehumanization* (e.g., Bandura 1990; Butler 2004; Fox and Levin 1998; Freire 1970; Kelman 1973; Young 2003). That conceptualization takes for granted that to be nonhuman is to risk being mistreated. The converse, humanization, entails familiarity, compassion, and understanding. The denigration of nonhumans goes unquestioned. It has no name, for nonhumans cannot logically be dehumanized. In general, nonhuman animals do not even enter into our discussion of harmful action.

Eviatar Zerubavel's work on mental filters is useful here. According to Zerubavel, across the life span we are socialized into particular ways of thinking and particular thoughts. He examines six main cognitive acts—perception, attention, classification, symbolizing, memory, and timing, of which attention and classification are most relevant to the process of reduction.

We pay attention and extend moral concern to certain beings, while others are considered "morally irrelevant" (1997, 39). Or, to use Susan Opotow's (1993) concept, they are beyond "the scope of justice." Philosophers call such treatment of non-humans speciesism, "the view that species is in itself a reason for treating some beings as morally more significant than others" (P. Singer 2006, 3). Because I am a member of a speciesist language community and want to be readily understood, I use speciesist terms in this chapter. I sometimes use the word "animals" to mean nonhuman animals, thus implying that humans are not animals. My solution is to qualify those animals as "non-human," which is hardly less problematic: I thereby collapse a variety of beings into a class whose defining characteristic is that they are not us. In the same way, "woman" qualifies "man." Man, like human, stands in for the universal being. The marginality of the Other is encoded in language.

Marginalization of nonhuman animals surfaced early in our research interviews. We launched each interview by asking participants how they would define harm, to which eighteen (nearly a third) offered definitions specifying or implying *human* victims. Likewise, sociologists have been little interested in nonhuman animals as subjects of any number of potentially germane inquiries (Arluke 2002). For example, scholars seem to mean harm to humans when they announce the importance of a "social harm perspective" (see Hillyard et al. 2004). Steve Tombs and Paddy Hillyard apply such a perspective to the issue of the overuse of antibiotics in factory farming: "It is now widely believed that this has created a situation in which certain bugs are now untreatable by modern medicine and that resistant super bugs are now spreading from poultry to humans" (2004, 49). In this statement the ultimate victim and object of concern is human.

Philosophers offer arguments that animals are essentially less-than. For example, Georges Bataille describes nonhuman animals' lack of consciousness. They do not transcend their experiences as humans do—or at least as far as we know. Bataille concedes, "Such a truth is negative, and we will not be able to establish it absolutely" (1989, 23). Scholars, of course, build their work on assumptions or premises that they hope their audiences will accept as plausible. That (some) nonhumans are unharmable is one such presumably plausible assumption.

Proper and Right Action

Research participants referred to a license to harm nonhumans owing to custom, utility, and religion. These discourses conferred legitimacy to their actions. They are widely used "permission slips," and their prevalence backs their effectiveness.

Custom

In appealing to custom, speakers emphasized that killing animals for meat has been going on for a long time and continues to be pervasive among multitudes. Mike said, "Humans have been eating meat since, we got on . . . ya know, since we've been on this planet, so." Tina stated, "As a culture it's just kind of . . . it's everywhere? Everybody does it. And so it's kind of easier to just say, 'Eh! Well. Not such a big deal.'" The collective mind here is a discursive, legitimating device to which some participants explicitly referred—such as by quoting the discourse, as Tina did.

In a variation, some said that meat eating was a personal habit. Mike cited the fact that he "grew up eating meat" as one basis for his doing so today. Robin likewise referred to "the way we grew up. It's what we're used to." Theresa described having been well socialized into her justification for meat eating: "We've always grown up believing that they were put on the planet to feed us." Whereas the time of growing up had passed in all cases for these adult research participants, the fact of having started eating meat before one made one's own decisions legitimized current conduct.

Utility

Most of our research participants railed against doing harm to animals for no reason. They objected to "just" inflicting pain. At the same time they commended the utility of killing nonhuman animals. Mike stressed, "I'm not gonna go shoot something an' just let it go, just let it go to waste." Although he is fine with hunting, Sam has "a problem with somebody catchin' something or killin' something and then just lettin' 'em die, be it Bambi or whatever." Rick, who hunts and fishes, stated, "I never hunted anything I didn't eat, so I don't believe in sport hunting. If you hunt, you eat what you kill." Brie denied that killing animals is harm, saying, "I think where the harm comes in is when people hunt for sport." In all cases the speakers expressed not wanting to harm per se, but rather wanting to eat meat: they desire the end result of harm. I return to the matter of desire momentarily, because I think it is a distinct logic—suffice it to say for now, a less thoughtful one than licensing based on utility. In the discussion of genocide in chapter 3, greed was a lure that speakers described as undermining self-control; it informed claims of powerlessness. Here, the achievement of some benefit licenses harmful action: it doesn't *require* it. Speakers emphasized the legitimacy of killing nonhumans on account of its use-value.

Religion

Religion gave several of our interviewees license to eat meat. Recall that these interviews were conducted in Tennessee, with persons mainly, though not exclusively, from that Bible Belt state. Religious license could be quite literal. Robin said, "I know that we have permission from God to eat [meat]." According to Theresa, "They were put on the planet to feed us." John added that God "wants us to eat them." Patty had a great deal of sympathy for nonhuman animals, had been vegetarian, and continued to avoid most meat. However, she shared,

"They eat fish in the Bible, so I eat fish." Caitlin said, "For the most part, I think that a lot of those animals have been . . . were created for us to *use*." Several research participants deconstructed these religious edicts in terms of nonhumans lacking souls and God's granting humans dominion over all other beings. I distinguish between a religious order, which confers power, and a natural order, in the face of which we humans have no choice.

NECESSITY OF THE HARM:
THE AGENT IS POWERLESS

Speakers used a variety of logics to emphasize their powerlessness not to harm the nonhumans they consume. These included the natural order, our physical survival, a physical inability to stop eating meat, and a personal or institutional inability to stop meat production.

Natural Order and Survival

The irreligious whom we interviewed emphasized a natural order instead of a supernatural one. George said a good deal about the "food chain," the fact that humans are "made to be omnivores" and the fact that "you shouldn't deny your nature." Brie said, "I mean, I'm a meat eater. I . . . I can't help it." Steve stated, "We are carnivores; that's our nature." Candy said, "I have teeth that are meant to eat meat." Susan naturalized human behavior in saying, "The circle of life constitutes some animals are bred to be nourishment." She erased human intention and presented animal consumption as inevitable with the expression "circle of life" and the passive construction of breeding ("are bred").

Such statements have academic backing. In their introduction to *Meat-Eating and Human Evolution*, Craig Stanford and Henry Bunn state, "There is little doubt that meat-eating became increasingly important in human ancestry, despite the lack of direct evidence in the fossil record of how meat was obtained, or how much was eaten, or how often, or how exactly increasing importance of meat-eating may have contributed to the rise of the genus *Homo*" (2001, 3). These authors maintain that meat eating was essential to human progress, thus our consumption was dictated by forces beyond us, despite "lack of direct evidence."

A related rhetoric to which speakers referred had to do with human survival:

INTERVIEWER: Do you eat meat?
EARL: Yes.
INTERVIEWER: Do you think that's harming an animal?
EARL: Not at all. It's survival. Yeah, I could care less about that.

Asked how she feels about killing animals for meat, Julianna equated meat eating with eating: "I think it's probably acceptable? Because people got to eat. You know, you have to eat." Ann commented, "Harming an animal . . . keeping them caged up . . . sometimes is a *necessity*." Tara addressed industrialized farming in particular: "If we didn't produce the meat the way we do, it would lead to starvation." Sam mentioned his personal survival: "After having gastric bypass surgery, I have to have my proteins." Sam also told a story of his daughter's fiancé hitting a deer while driving, "and if he was in a Toyota Camry it probably would have killed him 'cause it totaled the car." He concluded that "something has to be done" about deer overpopulation.

But most who channeled survival spoke rather abstractly, using common codes such as "It's eat or be eaten" (Beezer), "chain of life" (Alison), "circle of life" (Susan), and "food chain" (Michelle). In fact, speakers readily drifted from the logic of survival or even reversed it, as did Sam in this exchange:

INTERVIEWER: Do you really think we need cows to survive?
SAM: I believe . . . I believe we need . . . I believe we do. We [*sic*] believe we need beef and we need the milk. . . . I

understand we can . . . we can be vegetarians, but I think we're missing out, by doing so. I believe variety is the spice of life. And I love my steaks, I love fish . . . there's not too many things foodwise that I don't like.

Sam began his defense by affirming the necessity of meat and milk for survival but concluded with an assertion of individual preference. Prompted to critically evaluate their claims in the interviews ("Do you really think . . . ?") and permitted the space for elaboration, speakers were nimble users of discourses, even conflicting ones.

Can't Help It

Some research participants spoke of meat eating as something they did not want to do but that they did anyway. Tina was self-reflective: "It was more . . . more like, uh, my willpower caved. Um. And then it just slowly kinda crept back into my diet." Similar to appeals to natural order, the body simply rules. A variation on this "I can't help it" rhetoric had to do with powerlessness vis-à-vis the harm of institutionalized meat production. This logic took two rather different forms. Some research participants reasoned that the suffering imposed by the meat industries was necessary, as far as they could speculate. Alison offered that painfree killing of nonhuman animals is "just not economical, I guess." Susan said, "I'm guessing . . . that most of the time we . . . try to kill the animals humanely." A second expression of powerlessness had to do with one's individual inability to change the status quo. Sonia, for example, stated, "My refusal to eat it won't make a difference in whether or not they're killed." David stressed that "it would take a huge collective effort" to dismantle the factory farm industry. Thus, whereas some speakers conveyed trust in a well-intentioned system that tried not to harm but perhaps could not help *but* harm, others conveyed pessimism about changing the system.

Both groups acknowledge harm; the latter grapples with their own (ir)responsibility.

Once again, as in the case of genocide, harm agents convey a power paradox. They construct meat eating as right; they also succumb to it. Alleged power emboldens while alleged powerlessness undercuts responsibility. For hunters, the combined effect intoxicates. They enter the scene utterly unsure of how their story will end: do they control or are they altogether lacking in control (Presser and Taylor 2011)? Meat eaters are moved by a far more boring story of push and pull, although it entices no less. But grappling was probably a result of the provocation of the interview. In the moment, meat eating has a habitual, thoughtless quality, made easy by discourses that let us have it both ways and aided by the avoidance of knowledge, which I turn to next.

AVOIDING KNOWLEDGE

Only a few of those we interviewed were knowledgeable about the harms done to animals through factory farming. They trusted that factory-farmed animals were treated decently, without having any specific knowledge of such. Most failed to grasp the systemic nature of the abuse. When discussing animal abuse they tended to focus on individual wrongdoers, as when Don reasoned that learning what he had about factory farming "made [him] think twice about the persons . . . and the people that they have caring for the animals. I mean, should we just go around and kickin' 'em just because they're food?" John and Sam introduced the topic of football player Michael Vick's infamous dogfighting early on when asked their thoughts on harm to animals:

INTERVIEWER: Do you think that it's important that [animals] be treated humanely before they are slaughtered or does it matter? Are animals ours to do whatever we want with or do we need to respect them?

JOHN: Well, if . . . are you saying if you're raising them? For the purpose of the meat?

INTERVIEWER: Hmm . . . in any situation.

JOHN: Yeah, they need to be respected. I mean, for example, you know, look at what Michael Vick did with the dog-fighting type of thing, now that's . . . things like that . . . that's uncalled for. You don't need to be having private dog fights. That was definitely wrong.

INTERVIEWER: You ever heard stories about the inhumane . . . well, they're animals, so you can't treat them inhumanely, call it wrong . . . um, about the cruel way that animals are treated when they're . . . ?

SAM: Perfect example is Michael Vick, what he did with the dogs.

INTERVIEWER: Well I . . . just, right now, I'm talking about food.

By focusing on individual negative referents, Don, John, and Sam simultaneously minimized the phenomenon of animal harm and excused themselves from complicity. In fact, the vast majority of abuse is neither a matter of kicking animals nor one of using them for sport, but rather circumscribing life conditions that cause suffering—such as with severely limited space in which to move around while confined. We mystify animal abuse, a maneuver critical criminologists have documented concerning violence against humans (Box 1983; Reiman and Leighton 2009). We call attention to stranger rape, not the more common acquaintance rape; to street robbery, not robbery through corporate collusion. My data showcase the phenomenon at the micro level.

Meat eaters denied farmed animals' victim status (Sykes and Matza 1957) by ascribing complicity to them. Ali conjured cows as wanting to be harmed:

INTERVIEWER: Do you consider meat harm to the animals? Or meat eating?

ALI: Not really.

INTERVIEWER: Do you eat meat?

ALI: Yeah. I don' know [*chuckle*]. You look at some of the animals. Like I heard somebody describe cows as like you've never seen an animal more ready to die. Like all . . . there's just no life there. All they do is just walk, eat . . .

INTERVIEWER: Hmm.

ALI: . . . poop . . . grow meat [*chuckle*] and then that's it.

Ali equates "life" with recognizably human life, although not in those anthropomorphic terms. Failing to detect it among cows, she concludes that they must as much yearn to die as to live. The observation that nonhumans want to be killed is also suggested in corporate images compiled by animal rights activists for the web blog Suicide Food (2011). It is reminiscent of rape accounts in which victims allegedly want to be raped. Harm is not harm if victims desire it, and victims desire it on dubious evidence concerning how they are dressed, their failure to escape the situation, their mere presence in the setting for rape. The interests of the target are the same as those of the harm agent.

Our research participants did not seem to want to know about or to contemplate such harms, and they said so. Patty shared, "So, yeah, I like meat, and, yes, it's violent, but I try not to think about it when I eat meat. Every time I think about it, I'm so serious—I'll think about it and I'll stop eating meat for like three weeks." Steve denied knowledge of free range alternatives to factory-farmed meat:

INTERVIEWER: Do you ever go out of your way to buy free range meat or . . . ?

STEVE: If I was aware of that I would [buy it], but I'm not aware of that.

Steve also rejected the possibility that the interview itself was raising his awareness.

I too avoid knowledge of this category of harm when I am about to eat meat. Recently I wrote about putting "'animal suffering' out of [my] mind so quickly that [I am] not even aware of the move to resist thinking" (Presser and Taylor 2011, 487). Avoidance of knowledge is no trivial matter. For writer Geoffrey Wheatcroft (2011), refusal to know facts that are widely available "explains the woes of our time." Some view such refusal as avoidance of potentially psychologically upsetting information (e.g., Case et al. 2005). Lawrence Langer describes "the dilemma of digesting 'confirmed knowledge'" of the Nazi Holocaust (1997, 51): even the eventual victims had trouble taking in the reports of mass murder at the camps that were reaching the ghettos. He reasons that what is unthinkable is simply "a reality that we are unprepared to accept, because it either offends our sense of order or threatens to unravel the curtain before which we ply our daily lives" (52). Such denial runs on social factors, as Irene Bruna Seu explains in regard to human rights appeals: "It would be unproductive to look for an explanation of audiences' passivity simply in terms of an individuals' own psychological or emotional predisposition, or in their stated attitudes. . . . Instead, attention should be paid to what is socially and culturally available to the public to counteract the moral imperative contained within the appeals. It is also important to learn how wider cultural discourses . . . are employed" (2010, 454). In the present context refusal to know is facilitated by institutional arrangements that deal in signs both material (e.g., flesh already partitioned so that it doesn't look like flesh) and discursive (e.g., individual animals not so named). "The typical modern meat-eater prefers not to know how she came to eat that meat, and her wishes are obliged" (Presser and Taylor 2011, 487).

SIMPLE DESIRE

Twelve (one in five) of those we interviewed said that they eat meat because they like it: it tastes good. Another three mentioned its convenience: it is easy to eat meat. Philosopher

Charles Taylor contends that choosing actions simply on the basis of desire—"the inarticulate 'feel' of the alternatives" (1985, 24)—is characteristic of "the weak evaluator." In contrast, "the strong evaluator" judges the desires themselves as more or less desirable, consistent with the sort of person he or she wants to be. For Taylor, the "capacity for . . . strong evaluation is an essential feature of a person" (43). Charles Tilly likewise proposes that we humans should be able to appraise our desires because we are "reason-giving animals" (2006, 8). On these views the weak evaluator is lacking in full-fledged personhood.

Taylor (1985) suggests that some individuals simply lack the capacity for strong evaluation. Maybe so, but I found no such individuals among our research participants. All speakers were able to dig deeper and offer commentary on the bases for their desires when prompted to do so. Therefore, I have a different assessment of those who "just want to" eat meat than Taylor's. The words "I just want to" are a sort of protest against the question of why. Explaining *why* acknowledges that the actor has done something culturally wrong (Scott and Lyman 1968). In defying the need to explain why, the individual is not revealing a cognitive or social deficit: she is rejecting the implied illegitimacy of the action in question.

WHAT IS THE STORY?

Reflecting on his past meat eating, novelist Jonathan Safran Foer writes, "When I graduated [from college], I ate meat—lots of every kind of meat—for about two years. Why? Because it tasted good. And because more important than reason in shaping habits are the stories we tell ourselves and one another. And I told a forgiving story about myself to myself" (2009, 8). During interviews we heard few stories in the formal sense (i.e., a meaningful recapitulation of experience) of meat eating. Yet during some of the same interviews, research participants told stories of other wide-ranging harms on which they held varied positions: these harms included corporal punishment of children, war, state torture, and capital punishment. Recall that stories are devices for understanding and presenting ourselves as moral actors, autobiography being "the activity of explaining oneself" (Stone 1982, 10). As just discussed concerning "simple desire," speakers generally saw no need to account for the harm of meat eating. In fact, our interviews were deviant for treating the killing of some animals for meat as harm.

Charles Tilly writes, "When most people take reasons seriously, those reasons arrive in the form of stories" (2006, 95). Indeed, those who did question their complicity in harm to nonhumans told stories about it. An example is Tina, a one-time vegetarian, who recalled the following:

> There's something about the conditions of . . . of cows in . . . in a factory environment that I find quite awful, and, um . . . and the way they're . . . they're slaughtered I find quite awful. An' um, so I have a hard time eating that. But my in-laws one time bought a buffalo that . . . had lived on the open range and, ya know, they went in with a couple and they . . . got . . . they divvied up the buffalo. And . . . and I didn't have a problem eating that.

Tina's story is a simple one: her relatives purchased meat from a free-ranging animal; she ate it contentedly. But it fulfills the basic requirements of a story: A-then-B is recalled and a moral conclusion is drawn—that eating meat from an animal not made to suffer is okay.

Very different is Don, who resisted storytelling:

INTERVIEWER: Have you ever killed an animal yourself or taken part in the . . .

DON: Yes.

INTERVIEWER: . . . procedure?

DON: Yes.

INTERVIEWER: Can you tell me about that?

DON: Uh, well. We used to slaughter our own pigs. We used to slaughter our own cows. We used to slaughter our own chickens. Turkeys. I . . . I used to raise turkeys *myself* for food.

INTERVIEWER: And did you kill them?

DON: Yes.

INTERVIEWER: Do you mind telling me about that?

DON: Uh. I don't know . . . what do you . . . what do you want . . . what do you want to know?

INTERVIEWER: I mean, an example of the time you killed an animal . . . or times.

DON: Well, it just . . . during chicken season . . . we used to raise a hundred, a hundred and fifty chickens. So, yeah, we had to go around, catch the chickens, cut their heads off, and then . . . defeather 'em and clean 'em and get 'em ready to sell. The same with the pigs and same with the cows. It's all the same.

Don questions the meaning that the interviewer might want him to make of his participation in animal killing ("what do you want to know?"). His reminiscence "does not so much conclude as simply terminate" (White 1987, 16). He recalls actions in the past but they do not lead anywhere, and he makes no point, which stories and moral evaluations generally require.

Whether those who have no stories to tell are being defensive, I cannot say. Carol Adams suggests as much: "On an emotional level everyone has some discomfort with the eating of animals. . . . The intellectual framework of language that enshrouds meat eating protects these emotional responses from being examined" (1994, 66). What is clear is that meat eaters— and I include myself—make a moral compromise, whether or not they are fully aware of that moral compromise in the speaking moment. That speakers reject the need for storytelling reflects the prosaic acceptability of the harm in question, so the power paradox ("I am right to do this"; "I cannot act otherwise") goes down easy with speakers and listeners alike.

Speaking and Not Speaking
Animal Harm

Several global food revolutions have grown up in the past few decades, heightening awareness of the harms of factory farming and calling for local, slow, sustainable, and compassionate ways of feeding ourselves. It is sobering to learn that the language of animal harm may yet be resistant to those efforts, at least among some sectors of the population—and the meat industry. Arran Stibbe's (2001) analysis of publications produced by and for the meat industry reveals logics of harm, including references to animals as resources; the discourse of science, which naturalizes nonhumans' oppression; and nominalization of practices, which conceals human agency. The logics identified by my analysis track Stibbe's—specifically, the reduction of nonhumans and claims of power and powerlessness. The meat eaters whom we interviewed echoed institutional—corporate and academic—logics. The case of meat eating exposes the contribution that institutions make to commonly used discourses of harm, including their role in preventing certain realities from being spoken about and known. Corporate-cum-political arrangements nurture ignorance about the mistreatment of animals raised for human consumption. An especially bold instance of such nurtured ignorance is legislation passed in several U.S. states that makes it a crime to take pictures inside a slaughterhouse while undercover (Flynn 2012). One research participant, Scarlet, offered, "It's not that I try not to think about it; it's that I *don't have to* think about it."

The extreme and routinized reduction of nonhumans may explain the pervasiveness of harm to them. In addition, outsourced mistreatment allows us to blame someone else for whatever harms we *do* know about. The magnitude of the animal abuse enterprise invites claims that it cannot possibly be stopped. But speakers channeled other discourses, such as logics of license through appeal to natural or supernatural orders and claims of "not being able to help it," to explain their participation; these were not so obviously descended from the meat industry, although they may be used by that industry for advertising—the irresistible steak. Individuals are not mere spokespersons for powerful aggregates; they are agents who select among cultural discourses.

Perhaps, the reader might speculate, these discourses are simply ploys used to get away with satisfying one's preexisting motivation to do the harm. I doubt it. In my analysis simple desire was not enough. Besides, the claim that we act merely to achieve some end, that cultural accounts for such actions are therefore merely a felicitous resource after the fact, leaves entirely unanswered the questions: Why does one proceed to do *this* desired harm and not others? Why does *this* desire get satisfied? Rather than being a superficial or ad hoc aspect of action, legitimization—consisting in jargons of right to pursue one's desire and of helplessness before it—is at its heart.

CHAPTER 5

Intimate Partner Violence

A FAMILIAR STRANGER

HAVING JUST EXAMINED GENOCIDE and meat eating, we have visited the outermost margins of the field of criminology. Intimate partner violence (IPV), the focus of this chapter, is a much more typical object of criminological concern. It is a horrifically common sort of conventional violence. In the National Violence Against Women Survey of more than sixteen thousand men and women in the United States, 22.1 percent of the women and 7.4 percent of the men reported having experienced physical assault by a romantic partner. The survey determined that IPV accounts for most of the violence suffered by women in the United States (Tjaden and Thoennes 2000). Robert Thompson and colleagues (2006) arrived at an IPV prevalence rate of 7.9 percent in the prior year and 44 percent across one's lifetime, based on a sample of 3,429 U.S. women. A multinational survey of more than twenty-four thousand women in ten countries, sponsored by the World Health Organization, found that the lifetime prevalence of IPV, including physical or sexual assault, ranged from 15 to a shocking 71 percent (Garcia-Moreno et al. 2006).[1] Because IPV is most often a pattern of behavior rather than a one-time event, trauma and disruption can endure for lengthy periods (Rand and Saltzman 2003). All told, IPV causes a tremendous amount of suffering.

In this chapter I first revisit the question of the relationship between social distance and harm, scrutinized in chapter 2, which becomes especially problematic in regard to IPV. I make the case that certain discursively constructed cultural expectations of intimate partnerships promote the reduction of victims and consequently IPV. Especially relevant to IPV are expectations, discourses, and stories related to gendered power positions. The extreme division of male from female in societies and households most prone to IPV helps to resolve the contradiction suggested by the subtitle of this chapter—that of the familiar stranger. Second, I argue that, as with other types of harm, discourses of power and powerlessness promote IPV. In the case of IPV the violence promises to resolve a contradiction within a story of the relationship—that the rightfully empowered party is being deprived of power. As Jeff Hearn puts it, "Violence is an attempt to enforce that which is already not the case" (1998, 208). Hence too the bearing of Hannah Arendt's formulation, that violence and power are opposites: "Violence appears where power is in jeopardy" (1969, 56). Unlike these scholars, I am concerned with storied power and storied powerlessness. Thus, I maintain my focus on the constructed states of being that motivate harmful action.[2]

Empirical underpinning for this chapter's exploration comes mainly from thirty-eight studies published from 1979 to 2009 involving open-ended interviews with either batterers or with battering victims who recalled batterers' verbalizations (table 5.1). They represent all those I was able to locate that report qualitative accounts by offenders, first or secondhand, the latter recalled by victims. In all cases except one, abusers were male and their victims were female.[3] As shown in table 5.1, twenty studies included interviews with female victims only (some of which also involved staff interviews), nine with male perpetrators only, eight with both female victims and male perpetrators, and one with a man and a woman who were not a

TABLE 5.1

Intimate Partner Violence Studies and Sample Information

Author, Year	Sample specifics
Abraham (1999)	25 women recruited through social service organizations for battered South Asian women in three U.S. cities
Anderson and Umberson (2001)	33 men participating in a program for batterers in a southwestern city of the United States
Bergen (1995)	35 women who had obtained services from a battered women's shelter or rape crisis center
Bourgois (2003)	1 man and 1 woman (not a couple) involved in drug trafficking in New York City
Bui (2002)	16 victims of wife abuse, three social workers, and three community members, all immigrants to the United States from Vietnam
Burbank (1992)	Residents of an Australian Aboriginal community
Das Dasgupta and Warrier (1996)	12 women in contact with social service organizations for battered South Asian women
Dobash and Dobash (1979)	109 women in Scotland; otherwise unspecified
Draper (1992)	!Kung people of Botswana
Eisikovits (1996)	40 spouses (20 couples) in contact with local public social service agencies in Israel
Fernandez (1997)	15 young, married women who had received help from a women's center in Bombay, India
Gagné (1992)	3 women (plus informal, nonrecorded interviews with others, including 2 men) in a small, rural, central Appalachian community
Gilbert et al. (2001)	68 women, predominantly Latina and African American, interviewed in focus groups; recruited through methadone clinics and programs in New York City
Hattery (2009)	26 men and 32 women (8 of them couples) recruited from organizations for batterers and battered women in Minnesota and North Carolina

(continued)

TABLE 5.1
Intimate Partner Violence Studies and Sample Information
(continued)

Author, Year	Sample specifics
Hearn (1998)	60 men involved with the criminal justice system and batterers' treatment programs in the United Kingdom
Hegland (1992)	Women in Iran
Hydén (1995)	40 spouses (20 couples) in Stockholm, Sweden, based on involvement with police or social programs concerning violence
Hydén and McCarthy (1994)	40 spouses (20 couples) in Stockholm, Sweden, based on involvement with police or social programs concerning violence
Jones (1993)	9 women, victims of battering in the United States
Langford (1998)	30 women, victims of battering in the United States
Lewis et al. (2000)	142 women known to the court in Scotland
Mehrotra (1999)	30 Asian Indian immigrants, including abused and nonabused women, staff, and clients of battered women's support groups
Morash, Bui, and Santiago (2000)	33 women, intimate partner violence survivors of Mexican descent in Michigan
Mullaney (2007)	14 men in battering programs in mid-Atlantic United States
O'Connor (2000)	1 man who discussed his battering, in a sample of 19 incarcerated black men, at a maximum-security prison in Washington, DC
Presser (2008)	6 men who disclosed that they battered or were convicted of same, in a sample of 27 male perpetrators of violence; recruited through social service and correctional agencies in New York, New Jersey, Ohio, and Pennsylvania
Ptacek (1988)	18 men recruited through a Boston organization that counsels batterers

(continued)

TABLE 5.1

Intimate Partner Violence Studies and Sample Information
(continued)

Author, Year	Sample specifics
Purvin (2003)	1 woman battered by her boyfriend, the father of her four-year-old; recruited through community program for young mothers on welfare
Reitz (1999)	9 men, participants in a group for batterers
Renzetti (1992)	40 women battered by female partners; chosen for interviews from a sample of 100 who completed questionnaires
Riger, Raja, and Camacho (2002)	15 women, residents of urban domestic violence shelters
Rosen and Bird (1996)	1 man and 1 woman (a couple) in the United States
Short et al. (2000)	168 women (interviewed in focus groups); recruited by shelter directors, counselors, religious leaders, and women's organizations
Toby (1966)	1 man, incarcerated in a U.S. prison
Towns and Adams (2000)	20 women who had participated in support groups for battering victims in a large New Zealand city
Websdale (1998)	50 women, residents of a battered women's shelter, and 46 professionals involved with intimate partner violence in Appalachia
Wolf-Smith and LaRossa (1992)	50 women at a battered women's shelter
Wood (2004)	22 incarcerated men involved in a prison-based batterers' program in the southeastern United States

couple (Bourgois 2003). Finally, two ethno-anthropological studies did not provide information regarding the gender of informants.[4] All of these publications share accounts given after the abuse has taken place. But the fact that IPV is generally patterned behavior as opposed to a one-time incident lends some basis for suggesting that stories recounted in these interviews sustain the behavior even as they are after-the-fact verbalizations. A more vexing limitation is that they are select verbalizations filtered by authors. Because these statements are derived from secondary data, they can be suggestive only of the sorts of discourses that promote abuse; I use them to build theory and take a speculative stance.

SOCIAL DISTANCE, REDUCTION, AND INTIMATE PARTNER VIOLENCE

Violence against one's intimate partner poses a particular challenge to the idea that harmful action requires social distance. Romantic partners would seem to be close, sometimes even codependent or enmeshed. Often they have known each other for a long time. They share some or all of the following: a household, a bed, children, pets, money and other possessions, and a last name. Often they meet each other's basic needs. But intimate partners may at the same time be strangers. This estrangement derives from dominant cultural discourses that set out gendered positions. Let us explore this estrangement a bit.

Russell Jacoby views violence in general as a function of a fervent wish to maintain an identity unique from one's too-similar target. Whereas Jacoby treats that wish as a universal psychic need, he implicitly acknowledges its gendered nature. Concerning the importance of gender identity to men, he states that they "fear they will be stripped of their manliness; they worry about becoming effeminate. . . . The thousand rules, usually religiously based, that keep women apart from men— and sometimes keep them totally covered or hidden from men—bespeak this anxiety" (2011, 135). Jacoby does not explain why men must be different from women and why women do not face similarly stringent analogous requirements. He is hardly alone in these omissions. The idea that gender boundaries must not be crossed—and particularly that what is male must not be infiltrated by what is female—is cultural common sense, a premise of many cultural narratives including personal life stories and scholarly theories.

We know that gender hierarchy, in both household and society, is correlated with wife beating (Lateef 1992; McKee 1999; Mitchell 1992). Abusers claim to have rights and powers that their partners do not. They hold themselves to different norms of sexual behavior (e.g., monogamy), paid labor, domestic labor, and social life than they hold their victims. Jamie Mullaney summarizes her interviews with male batterers: "Men's right to limit the movement of the bodies of women— sexually or otherwise—comes with the parallel right of unrestricted movement of their own bodies" (2007, 241). Hank, a research participant in Angela Hattery's sample of abusers and abuse victims, admitted to infidelity "and yet would not tolerate any suggestion of the same by his girlfriend" (2009, 141). However intimate they may be, women and men are constructed as different in these partnerships. In fact, the presence of intimacy—at least as mutual understanding—is questionable. Jody Miller writes, "A great deal of research has shown that men who engage in violence against women report 'a lower capacity for empathy' than nonaggressive men" (2008, 218). Women interviewed by Elaine Weiss (2004) reported that their abusive partners often called them "bitch" and "whore" before or while assaulting them. Abusers construct their victims as markedly different from themselves. Their boundary work receives support from broader discourses of extreme gender difference.

Differentiating oneself from victims is not all or only about putting them down. Perpetrators diminish themselves as well. They become the mirror image of the victim, as they strive for ownership. Furthermore, when not being beaten, victims may be admired, even revered. The duration of such admiration may be short—a so-called honeymoon period in cycles of abuse—or lengthy. Cultural codes of chivalry, allegedly putting women "on a pedestal," which includes protecting them and making symbolic protective gestures, explain such veneration. These codes are by no means incompatible with doing harm to women. Responding to discussions of whether women benefit from chivalrous treatment, Jackson Katz writes, "What lurks just beneath the surface of the debate about chivalry is the question of men's ownership of women and the historical reality that for centuries, men have controlled women by force" (2006, 55). Thus, one of Hattery's research participants, an abuse victim named Candy, described the chivalrous premise of her abusive partnership: "He might try to hit me and he might try to kill me but. . . . *He was going to protect me from everybody else*" (2009, 38; emphasis in original). That revering one's target does not preclude harming them is also indicated by cases of human sacrifice (Girard 1977, 95) and hunting where prey are conceived as grand and majestic (Presser and Taylor 2011). In each case the target is a caricature. Although vastly different from the harm agent, targets are not unique unto themselves.

IMPETUS TO HARM:
A POWER PARADOX

The impetus to do violence begins with a discursive power paradox. Batterers are supposed to rule their partner. Yet they are powerless: their power and privilege are thwarted by the victim, other individuals, or larger forces. They must use violence to overcome a threat to their identity, or they lose control over violence, which they reify and outsource. "Can" and "must" congeal to form a narrow conclusion: strike out.

Across accounts drawn from qualitative research on IPV, perpetrators identified three main causes of their violence: a loss of self-control, often due to inebriation; the victim's provocation; and perpetrators' resistance to the victim's control efforts. Less often they spoke of sexual jealousy; a need to defend against the victim's violence; a desire to control the victim; and the use of violence to communicate, especially when verbal communication was not working. In two studies abusers reported that they were violent because of a felt need to retaliate against victims for something they had done (Ptacek 1988; Rosen and Bird 1996). Victims of IPV told interviewers that their partners attributed their battering to loss of self-control, the victim's provocation, desire to control, resistance to being controlled, anger over the target's ingratitude toward them, the abuser's inebriation from alcohol, and the instigation of the family of origin. Thus, abusers stressed power to abuse and powerlessness to act otherwise.

A License to Strike Out

Verbalizations suggesting a license to beat one's partner were evident across accounts. The majority of Julia Wood's interviewees (eighteen of twenty-two) expressed the view that "a man is entitled to use violence to discipline his female partner(s)" (2004, 563). Likewise in Joseph Vandello and Dov Cohen's study of honor cultures, "the view that men can sometimes use violence and women should sometimes tolerate it" prevails (2003, 1008). Particular expressions of license to abuse follow:

> I felt she was a possession of mine, that I owned her. That's why I felt motivated to be violent towards her and not to anyone [else]. (Hearn 1998, 127)

> I've always liked to dominate, get everything my own way. I might be sort of tempted to say familiarity, you know, sort of, I know you're not going to leave me, so I can crack you as much as I want sort of thing. (Hearn 1998, 135)

Victims did not meet certain expectations:

> Until we were married 10 years or so there was no violence or anything. But then after a while, it just became, it just became too much. . . . I don't know if I demanded respect as a person or a husband or anything like that, but I certainly, you know, didn't think I was wrong in asking not to be filled up with fatty foods. (Ptacek 1988, 147)

A couple more incidents happened over the next year . . . where I did strike her, and for basically the same reason. I just tried making love, and making love, and she couldn't do it. (Ptacek 1988, 147)

He thought it was an insult to him to slam the door; he got in, opened the door and beat me. (Morash, Bui, and Santiago 2000, 81)

As long as I keep my mouth shut and I'm, like, seen but not heard, everything's okay. (Purvin 2003, 1270)

Whereas abusers may direct victims' behavior, the reverse does not hold:

I don't think I used to like to be confronted about being high [on heroin], even though I was high. And it would bother me. It bothered me to a point where I would strike out. (Ptacek 1988, 148)

I think a lot of it had to do with my frustration of not being able to handle children. You know, they'd tell me to shut up. "You're not going to tell me to shut up." And then [my wife] would tell me, you know, "Let me handle this." I said, "I'm the man of the house." (Ptacek 1988, 147)[5]

Gestures by victims that abusers construed as controlling them were met with violence. Established positions within the relationship ("man of the house") were licensing devices. The earlier discussion of chivalry pertains. It is the man's prerogative to control the other members of the household physically, socially, and economically.

The Powerless Protagonist

Abusers also, and very often, spoke of violence as determined by some external force, a logic captured by one of James Ptacek's (1988) respondents: "it just became too much."

He would say, "Look, this isn't me. It's the drink that is making me act this way." (Dobash and Dobash 1979, 188)

He always swore his parents ordered him to do it. (Hegland 1992, 211)

An abuser in Jeff Hearn's study described self-defense in strong, apparently figurative terms:

> It isn't if things go wrong, it's the matter if they try to clinch me into a tight corner, you know I must bust out of that corner before they try to get me penned in there. It's just. I don't know, it's natural instinct I think. I won't be told by anybody, put it that way. And the violence starts like that. . . . I mean I just stick up for myself, and I don't see no violence in it actually. (Hearn 1998, 118)

According to Gresham Sykes and David Matza's (1957) neutralization theory, this abuser is denying the victim, positioning her as an assailant. Deeper probing of this excerpt reveals subsurface linguistic features that are of interest. First, the appeal to natural instinct and the metaphors of being cornered and trapped give way to claims of the unwilled, unthinking necessity of escape by any means. Second, the speaker nominalizes violence, treating it as a thing ("it's natural instinct"). Norman Fairclough explains, "Nominalization turns processes and activities into states and objects, and concretes into abstracts. . . . [It] entifies a local and temporary condition into an inherent state or property" (1992, 182–183). The violence becomes an entity from which the violator stands at a remove. Third, the speaker twice uses "just," which simplifies his actions: they are *mere* manifestations of instinct and self-defense. Fourth, and germane to the power paradox, the speaker articulates a principle informing his violence: "I won't be told by anybody." *Either* he attacks out of natural instinct *or* he attacks on account of a code that says he should not be told what to do, but both cannot be true.

Powerlessness may be spoken of as a temporary state produced by the situation one is in. Critical criminological perspectives such as structured action theory (Messerschmidt 1993) theorize an elevated risk of male violence when men lose social and economic power. Hoan Bui quotes one abuse victim recalling, "My husband was not happy with his life in the United States because he experienced a decline in social status and power" (2004, 99). Darren in Angela Hattery's study contextualizes his abuse in terms of diminished economic power after internal migration: "I was making a lot less money than I was in Washington State. And I was contributing a lot less to the household. . . . I didn't feel like I was the man of the house, you know" (2009, 89). Threats to the breadwinner position in the household are conditioned by race, culture, socioeconomic class, and historical conditions. These tangibly impinge on opportunities. But IPV occurs *across* lines of race, ethnicity, socioeconomic status, and historical periods because it is the threats that abusers construct, and not real threats, that animate harm.

Scholars have not adequately acknowledged how much *helplessness* is written into the state of being "a man" in our culture. Idealized gender relations cultivate the vulnerability inherent in dominant standards of masculinity, as novelist Alice Munro's protagonist Sophia observes, "They would be displeased to have anybody call them docile, yet in a way they are. They submit themselves to manly behavior. They submit themselves to manly behavior with all its risks and cruelties, its complicated burdens and deliberate frauds" (2009, 294). That construction of masculine submission is comparable to Matza's mood of fatalism. Discussed in the context of genocide, the mood of fatalism is a "sense of irresponsibility" (1964, 89) that permits criminal behavior. Matza describes its gendered character: "The mood of fatalism is the negation of the sense of active mastery over one's environment. It is likely to culminate in a sense of desperation among persons who place profound stress on the capacity to control the surroundings. Such a stress is implicit in customary precepts that celebrate the virtues of manliness" (189). Because the hegemonic version of masculinity is tied to control and because control is elusive, a *lack* of control is in the nature of hegemonic masculinity. Matza implies that the mood of fatalism is conjured discursively, for it is a type of neutralization (188). I would emphasize even more than Matza that actors *signify themselves into* this mood. They cast themselves as protagonists of stories where especially manly heroes fight against that which ensnares them because it is right to do so.

The inevitability of harm is underscored in statements that emphasize the abuser's rage. Both IPV perpetrators and victims referred to perpetrators' anger. When perpetrators did so, they emphasized their anger as inevitably leading to violence. They described a schism between mind and will, and body and action. They used language depicting an utter lack of presence in the moment of violence, to the point where many implied an altered neurological state—material, mysterious, and transitory:

Just like completely lose it, and go completely over the top. (Gadd 2000, 436)

It all boils up like a volcano, it's waiting. (Hearn 1998, 123)

I could kill her because what it is, is when I'm beating the wife, I don't know what I'm doing. My mind just goes blank, I go berserk. (Hearn 1998, 142)

When I got violent, it was not because I really wanted to get violent. It was just because it was like an outburst of rage. (Ptacek 1988, 143)

A blowout is where I lose, I just lose everything. I would just blank out, more or less. You know, like there would be this gap in between where I wouldn't actually remember. You know, like all I could remember seeing is like white,

little twinkling white, red, like lights. That's all I can
remember. That's a blowout. (Ptacek 1988, 144)

My heart would feel like it would jump up slap out of my
chest. You know, everything gets blurry at that time. My
heart's racing and I might start twitching. I lose my focus.
Maybe it's endorphins or something because, because it was
almost a high. It was almost a high. I would get dizzy from
it, it would just be so intense. (Reitz 1999, 157)

Well, I don't know how to explain. . . . You see, in our
heads there is a place with two poles. There has to be a certain distance between them. When you get angry, you get
close to one of the poles. In my head, the poles are too close
together, so that when I get angry, they crash into each
other. I can see from you that you don't believe me, but it
is in fact true. A doctor himself told me this. I think it was
caused by a motorcycle accident I was in. I simply get a total
blackout. (Hydén 1995, 67–68)

John Dollard and colleagues' (1939) frustration–aggression
hypothesis accounts for these so-called outbursts and blowouts.
The hypothesis states that frustration of one's goals provokes an
aggressive drive that stirs violence. Michael Gottfredson and
Travis Hirschi (1990) explain criminal behavior as a function of
having failed to develop sufficient self-control in early childhood. Their subject is a more calculating individual than is
Dollard's, not riled up and not so much driven as conditioned
for misconduct given the opportunity.

In general, though, scholars are skeptical of the idea that
violence is beyond an individual's control. Walter DeKeseredy
asks, "If these men have terrible problems with self-control,
how do they manage to keep from hitting people until they are
home alone with their loved ones?" (2011, 61). Instead
DeKeseredy emphasizes social causes including peers, pornogra-
phy, and misogynist attitudes. David Gadd and Tony Jefferson

treat abusers' statements to the effect that they couldn't help their violence as subterfuge, possibly unconscious, for the real, psychic causes of violence. The rationalization masks an "unarticulated desire to be free of the kind of disturbing knowledge that we know to be true but cannot accept." They recommend getting "behind the excuses and rationalizations men make for assaulting their partners to expose the unhappiness they mask" (2007, 158). These works offer quite different understandings of self-control and violence, but they all turn our attention to the "real" issues: drive, personality, environment, and anxiety. In contrast, the current approach is oriented toward cultural discourses concerning all of these factors, which promote violence.

TWO SHORT STORIES

Two men, Vaughan and Harry, told stories of committing lethal or near-lethal violence against their wives (Booker 1994; Presser 2008). Their stories convey a power paradox. The most palpable theme of both stories is powerlessness—of being overcome. Vivid metaphors aided in these constructions of powerless states. More latent in their stories is a theme of power—the discourse of male entitlement. Victims' disregard of that power legitimizes the protagonists' violence.

Seeing Red (Vaughan)

I was coming home in the early hours of the morning, pretty intoxicated. On approaching my home I saw a man coming down the steps, apparently leaving our house. I went upstairs and found Gail awake, sitting on the edge of the bed, smoking a cigarette. I asked her about the man.

> "Who was the dude I saw leaving?"
> "What are you talking about?"
> "You know what I mean. Who was he?"
> "Your son's father."

It was as if I had been hit over the head with a baseball bat. You've heard the saying "see red." Well I saw red. Every possible hidden or dark emotion that I had came to the surface. I remember the flash, the anger. (Booker 1994, 69)

Going Ballistic (Harry)

HARRY: Uh [*laughs*], somebody had told me—called me from work—and told me that they had seen my wife transporting people around in my car. And, uh, I just kind of went ballistic. And when she showed up, I went down this long, dead-end, hollow type of place, and at the time I was going, I was going about 75 or 80 miles an hour? I reached over and opened the door and tried to push her out the car. That's how fuckin' mad I was [*chuckles*]. But, y-you know, sh . . . in the end . . . when she held on, when the car stopped, that's when she shot me.

LO: She had a gun?

HARRY: Yeah. She had my gun.

LO: Mm-hmm? Mm-hmm?

HARRY: [*Takes a drink.*]

LO: And . . . did you go to the hospital?

HARRY: Yeah. Yeah I did.

LO: In that situation, so you were trying to . . . push her out the car door . . .

HARRY: Mm-hmm, I was really pissed about what had . . .

LO: . . . trying to kill her or trying to . . . ?

HARRY: Trying to kill her would probably be a more accurate statement.

In both stories the mandate of female fidelity licenses murder (only one man succeeds) that is nonetheless out of the protagonist's control, so enraged is he. The lack of control is amply described while the mandate is simply implied. Storytellers take for granted understandings they supposedly share with audiences: the more socially entrenched the understandings, the less these understandings seem to require articulation.

Constructing the Reduced Other: Same-Sex IPV

If IPV is gendered, what shall we make of violence in same-sex relationships? Its incidence is reportedly as high as or even higher than that of heterosexual couples (Elliot 1996; Messinger 2011; Renzetti 1992). It might be said that partners in same-sex relationships characterized by battering "do" masculinity and femininity (West and Zimmerman 1987). That is, they enact traits associated with these poles of socialized existence, and thus the person doing masculinity ipso facto does aggression. For the sake of a general theory of harm, however, I find it more useful to center theoretical attention on the power paradox. Gender constructs that paradox but so too do other ideologies.

Lynn Chancer's perspective helps greatly here. Chancer calls attention to sadomasochism as a pervasive but not necessarily erotic dynamic in human societies. The sadomasochistic dynamic encourages the "establishment of a hierarchical division between self and other that rests on the attribution of superiority to the sadist and of inferiority to the masochist" (1992, 55). According to Chancer, the sadomasochistic dynamic characterizes relations under capitalism and patriarchy. Despite the connection between sadomasochism and patriarchy, "women are quite capable of acting sadistically for a variety of reasons and under differing sets of circumstances, while men are quite capable of adopting a range of masochistic behavior" (33). A society that nurtures sadomasochism by virtue of gender or any other sort of oppression nurtures sadomasochism in general. As Chancer states, "one learns to take these roles within the context of a particular society, in this case, an arguably sadomasochistic one" (194).

Claire Renzetti's interviews with battered lesbians reveal power positions in their abusive romantic relationships (see

1992, 48–49), similar to those seen in heterosexual relationships: "I'd clean the house, cook dinner, and she'd come home and I'd have everything all ready. She'd come through the door and say, 'What'd you do all day, sit home?' She knew I had been at work all day" (52). This abusive partner assumes the prerogative to mock the victim's contribution to the household. Even where partners do not assume traditional gender roles, asymmetrical power arrangements may prevail and so too stories of one's partnership characterized by the power paradox. The abuser has the right to dominate the victim, including by violence, but violence is also beyond the abuser's control. "Insecurities got him a lot" (Cruz and Firestone 1998, 168): he is a captive.

STORIES THAT STRUCTURE
HARM TO INTIMATES

Perpetrators of IPV reduce their partners and themselves. These constructions build on cultural discourses that pertain to power. Batterers may be emotionally close with their victims but the relationship is structured to limit identification with and thus to reduce them. In addition, the batterer is inspired by a storied power paradox. Whereas IPV perpetrators notoriously emphasize their masculine power and privilege as against the victim's feminine subordination, they also construct themselves as lacking power, momentarily or otherwise. Some psychoanalytic and anthropological accounts wed this paradoxical self-construction to the reality of a powerful maternal figure; some such accounts risk normalizing violence against women. They also neglect the conventional character of male vulnerability, which is fastened to habits of speech. Barely being able to control one's emotions, including anger and sexual passion, is well within the parameters of hegemonic masculinity.

Other sociologists have remarked on abusers' incoherent explanations for abuse (e.g., Hearn 1998, 133). Against dominant notions of meaning as requiring coherence, here incoherence—the essence of the harm-promoting power paradox—makes the point and animates action. The power paradox may provoke the batterer emotionally. Whether the violence is impassioned or calculated, though, it promises to resolve the power paradox.

Like other sorts of harm, this one runs on social support. The abuser's prior exposure to violence is exposure to gender-based reductions and to the storied power paradox. In the present one's peers condone or egg on the reduction of women to resources for sexual release. Peers also confirm the logics of entitlement and loss of control. Victims may support the power paradox by chiding abusers on their success or failure in the masculine role. Institutions also license abuse through tolerance in the form of omissions and specifications. Consider, for example, the various marital exemption statutes that reduce victims of marital rape to "wives" (Siegel 1995). These statutes require that women who seek legal relief for marital rape present evidence of brutality or separation. The decisions of criminal justice agents (e.g., police, judges) traditionally have supported the logic of the inevitability of male-perpetrated IPV, hence nonintervention by police officers, mitigation in charging, and lenient sentencing. The influence of these external supports testifies to the social foundations of IPV, which consist in compelling stories that set out who people are and what they must (not) and can (not) do in particular moments of their lives.

CHAPTER 6

Penal Harm

STIGMA, THREAT, AND RETRIBUTION

A HARM THAT ENJOYS WIDESPREAD if not universal support in modern societies is that which the state imposes on persons it deems criminals, or *penal harm* (Clear 1994). The U.S. penal harm project stands out internationally. Our nation's incarceration rate is the highest in the world (ICPS 2012). More than 2.2 million Americans—disproportionately blacks and Hispanics—were incarcerated in 2011 (Glaze and Parks 2012). More than 1 in 100 adults are behind bars, although that statistic obscures even more striking race specifics: 1 in 9 black men ages twenty to thirty-four and 1 in 36 Hispanic men are serving time (*New York Times* 2008). Whereas the imprisonment rate declined from 2009 to 2011 (Carson and Sabol 2012; Guerino, Harrison, and Sabol 2011) following steep increases in the 1980s and 1990s (Justice Policy Institute 2000), the length of the average prison stay has risen 36 percent over 1990 levels (Pew Center 2012). The foregoing numbers say nothing about the torture of solitary confinement made routine in the supermax facilities that now operate in forty-four states (AFSC 2012). As journalist Adam Gopnik (2012) observes: "The scale and the brutality of our prisons are the moral scandal of American life." The United States is the only Western nation that uses the death penalty. A total of 1,296 persons have been executed since the death penalty was reinstated nationwide in 1976 (DPIC 2012a). Besides incarceration and execution, we socially and politically marginalize convicts long after they have served their sentence. Persons with a past felony conviction encounter deep discrimination in employment, housing, education, public benefits, and political participation. The harmful effects of discriminatory practices cause harm to convicts as well as their families and their communities.

This chapter asks, why do we inflict—and support—penal harm? My answer is based on examples with U.S. particulars. I hope that the United States will serve as a strong case with which to forge a general theory. In addition, I hope to shed light (though more definitive word awaits comparison with other nations) on the U.S. exceptionalism reflected in the data. Why do we punish with such abandon? I argue that a *story* of penal harm fuels it and that the especially contradictory American version of the story fuels a whole lot of it. Note, though, that my basic argument applies just as well to the minimalist approach that some, myself included, would take to punishing serious offenders. My purpose is to explain harm generally, and not just harm that many think of as excessive or preventable.

I draw on two main sources of data, qualitative interviews and court cases. Thirty individuals in Tennessee were asked to discuss their attitudes concerning a variety of harmful practices, including incarceration and execution. These interviews have been described in earlier chapters. Twelve, or 40 percent, opposed the death penalty, higher than observed in national surveys (for 2011), which put death penalty opposition in the range of 27 to 31 percent (DPIC 2012b).[1] Despite such views, no one we interviewed opposed imprisonment. That is, everyone supported penal harm under some circumstances. We also analyzed U.S. Supreme Court cases evaluating the merits and limits of penal harm. Using the database CQ Supreme Court Yearbook, a research team collected information on all cases heard from the

2000–2001 term to the most recent available term, 2010–2011, that addressed criminal law and procedure—a total of 308 cases. We examined each of these and selected twelve cases in which the Supreme Court justices debated the warrant of doing harm by way of criminal justice (see table 6.1). Other cases did not offer such philosophical debates. Nine of the twelve court cases attended to the validity of the death penalty; the three others concerned imprisonment or prison conditions. All but two cases (*Smith v. Texas* and *Begay v. United States*) grappled with the U.S. Constitution's Eighth Amendment prohibiting "cruel and unusual punishment."[2]

CONTRASTING CHARACTERS

The Eighth Amendment anchors the story that casts the state's harm as altogether different from both revenge and the criminal's harm. Linguist Livia Polanyi discerned elements of "the American story," including the logic that "causing pain is wrong and wrongdoing should be punished by pain" (1985, 136). Although that may serve as a fundamental logic in U.S. society, it is highly selective. Not all pain caused by humans is judged as wrong. Chapter 4, for example, made clear that pain visited on nonhuman animals is generally accepted. We also typically exclude from opprobrium acts of so-called justifiable homicide depending on both the agent of homicide and the victim: for example, suspected offenders may be justifiably murdered at the hands of police. And penal harm was generally cast as good in both U.S. Supreme Court decisions and the remarks of citizens. In fact, several of those we interviewed seemed confused or expressed defiance when the interviewer cast punishment as harm. Earl responded somewhat caustically to the question "Is punishing criminals an acceptable harm?": "That's a whole 'nother word than harm then. You were done with the harm." The moral acquittal of penal harm (and other state violence) brings us to the question that Todd Clear poses in his

TABLE 6.1
Select Court Decisions

Case	Year	Background	Decision
Penry v. Johnson	2001	Penry was sentenced to death in Texas.	Instructions to jury regarding how to weigh mitigating factors (mental retardation and child abuse victimization) in capital sentencing must be clear.
Atkins v. Virginia	2002	Atkins was sentenced to death in Virginia but contended he was mentally retarded and hence could not be sentenced to death.	Death penalty should not be imposed on mentally retarded defendants.
Porter v. Nussle	2002	Nussle, a Connecticut prisoner, alleged harassment and assault by corrections officers.	The Prison Litigation Reform Act must be the first resort for all prisoner grievances, whatever they concern, before filing suit.
Ring v. Arizona	2002	Ring faced the death penalty in Arizona.	The defendant in a capital case has a right to a jury trial for determining aggravating factors.
Ewing v. California	2003	A California court sentenced Ewing to twenty-five years to life in prison for felony grand theft, under that state's three-strikes law.	The three-strikes law does not violate the Eighth Amendment; the lower court's decision was upheld.
Roper v. Simmons	2005	Simmons was sentenced to death in Missouri for murder committed when he was seventeen.	The death penalty is barred for persons under eighteen years old at the time of their offense.

(continued)

TABLE 6.1
Select Court Decisions (continued)

Case	Year	Background	Decision
Kansas v. Marsh	2006	The Kansas Supreme Court determined that the death penalty in that state was unconstitutional due to lack of clarity regarding the balance of aggravating and mitigating factors.	The Kansas death penalty statute is constitutional.
Panetti v. Quarterman	2007	Panetti was sentenced to death in Texas and claimed incompetency to be executed, which Texas courts rejected.	Procedural requirements to hear evidence of incompetency for death penalty—in this case due to mental illness—were not followed.
Smith v. Texas	2007	Smith was sentenced to death in Texas and held that jury instructions were flawed.	The Texas death penalty court procedure (as in Penry v. Johnson 2001) was flawed: Smith need not show egregious harm due to procedural problem.
Baze v. Rees	2008	Baze and Bowling were each sentenced to death in Kentucky for double homicide and claimed that the lethal injection protocol for execution violated the Eighth Amendment.	Kentucky's lethal injection protocol is not unconstitutional.
Begay v. United States	2008	Begay was arrested for a felony in New Mexico and had several prior convictions including DUIs, which placed him at risk of a mandatory fifteen-year prison term for three or more prior convictions for certain drug crimes or violent felonies.	DUI is not a violent felony.
Kennedy v. Louisiana	2008	Kennedy raped his eight-year-old stepdaughter, for which Louisiana sentenced him to death.	Death penalty may not be used in nonhomicide cases.

study of penal harm: "Why . . . does the government get to do what its citizens cannot?" (1994, 8).

Regarding the construction of illegal versus legal violence during capital trials, Austin Sarat distinguishes these discourses: "While the violence outside the law is unnecessary, irrational, indiscriminate, gruesome, and useless, law's violence, the violence of the death penalty, is described as rational, purposive, and controlled through values, norms, and procedures external to violence itself" (1993, 54). Speakers verbalized this dichotomy when they described violent crime as cruel and criticized legal violence that does not in their view adhere to standards of rationality and utility. But they departed from the dichotomy when they also conceptualized criminal violence as calculated—not irrational at all.

Others we interviewed endorsed "an eye for an eye" retribution where punishment should be precisely as cruel as the offender's act of violence—even identical to it. As such, and as Judith Kay (2005) points out, punishers are not so pure, and their project is not necessarily about transcending the original offense. A distinction drawn by Joseph Campbell, who famously conceptualized the mythic hero, is important here: "Typically, the hero of the fairy tale achieves a domestic, microcosmic triumph, and the hero of myth a world-historical macrocosmic triumph. Whereas the former—the youngest or despised child who becomes the master of extraordinary powers—prevails over his personal oppressors, the latter brings back from his adventure the means for the regeneration of his society as a whole" (1949, 37–38). Theresa, one research participant, channeled the theme of macrocosmic triumph: "To protect the thousands, you have to do something with this one." Others expressed broad goals concerning justice. But moral transcendence and thus macrocosmic triumph were frequently abandoned in favor of the microcosmic variety—either a workmanlike criminal justice apparatus that did well enough or a system that did what it could to exact revenge for the victim's family. Speakers' identification with heroism was solid but terrifically supple.

If the moral distinction between punishers and offenders is somewhat messy, the punishers and their harm projects are nonetheless more complex than offenders and *their* projects. In *Kennedy v. Louisiana,* which bars use of the death penalty in cases other than murder, the court characterized the punisher as abiding by "standards of decency" while the project of the adversary is "moral depravity" (referring to the *Coker v. Georgia* decision).[3] In addition, the guidelines of the punisher-hero are ever-evolving, whereas the offender's calculations are based on a static drive or desire. Justices in the *Baze v. Rees* decision affirmed the state's "earnest desire to provide for a progressively more humane manner of death."[4] However flexible, the hero's guidelines must be "objective" and must adhere to a "measured, normative process."[5] In *Penry v. Johnson* the court determined that instructions to the jury concerning how to reason about mitigating factors in death penalty cases were unclear. "At best, the jury received mixed signals." Those mixed signals undermined the proper characterization of penal harm agents—that they summon a "reasoned moral response" to evidence. In *Roper v. Simmons* disqualification of the warrant to execute turned on the existence of an observed "national consensus" against putting juvenile offenders to death.[6] The gesture toward a national consensus is symbolic of the methodical and democratic process that the "good" agent of harm undertakes.

But the process is *not* methodical. It is no secret that, as a matter of course, we limit the imposition of pain in striking plea agreements with convicts. Plea bargains have the state relinquishing some of its power to punish and thus the moral aspect of the gesture. Even when endorsing retribution, speakers acknowledged the moral compromises of doing penal harm. What is the nature of a penal harm project that dramatizes both moral condemnation and marketlike practicality?

REDUCTION THROUGH
STIGMATIZATION

Agents of penal harm reduce their target. Recall from chapter 2 that to reduce a target is (1) to characterize the target in terms of very few interests or (2) to deny that the target has unique interests, distinguishable from others, including the perpetrator. The former is relevant in the case of penal harm. Speakers denied the complexity of those who commit crimes. They characterized them as having little else going on *except* crime.

Everett Hughes first developed the concept of a master status as one that "tends to overpower, in most crucial situations, any other characteristics which might run counter to it" (1945, 357). Howard Becker later noted, "The status of deviant (depending on the kind of deviance) is this kind of master status. One receives the status as a result of breaking a rule, and the identification proves to be more important than most others. One will be identified as a deviant first, before other identifications are made" (1963, 33). We found, in our interviews, even more radical reductions where the target of penal harm is constructed as harm itself. Thus, Matt referred to certain offenders not as harmful but rather as "a harm to society." Don explained the "necessity" of execution: "You're taking out the bad part—or the bad person—that could do more harm than just the one act." A bad person stands little chance of being appreciated as a complex person, a "bad part" even less.

In the penal harm story, the offender is all bad and only bad. The idea of the "born criminal" has roots in Cesare Lombroso's 1876 book *L'Uomo Delinquente* [Criminal Man]. That designation is applied selectively. Speakers—those we interviewed and judges whose written opinions we analyzed—distinguished between hardened criminals and a more redeemable type. Ann asserted that "there's different levels of criminals." Gabriella likewise noted, "Of course you may rehabilitate certain—I think there are some people, they're just so sick in the head, they may never be able to be rehabilitated, but there are others who *could* be." The irredeemable are "career criminals" and "habitual offenders."[7] Youth are often presented as exemplars of the redeemable offender, possessing the "potential to attain a mature understanding of [their] own humanity."[8] Jane articulated the common sense that criminals become hardened—beyond reform—as they age: "After a certain point I think maybe all we can do is just keep 'em penned up—unfortunately?" The offender's essence comes to be fixed. For the sake of comparison, we might consider the non-reductive way that Jane spoke about offenders and punishment. Jane's critique of reduction is suggested in her disapproval of three-strikes laws. In lieu of these laws, which mandate life imprisonment upon one's third felony conviction, she endorsed case-by-case evaluation where "people make a decision about other people based on individual circumstance." Jane was unusual in calling both offenders and their punishers "people."

Several speakers alleged that convicts were not productive or contributing members of society, thereby reducing them to their function. For example, Earl asked, rhetorically, "Why should we feed 'em? What good are they to us?" A related discursive strategy, used by only three research participants with very similar wording, was to endorse the death penalty on the basis of there not being "a reason" to keep the targets alive. The message is that persons are permitted to live only insofar as they have a purpose, and persons who have broken a law are presumed to have no purpose. As Michelle Alexander observes, "Like the 'coloreds' in the years following emancipation, criminals today are deemed a characterless and purposeless people" (2010, 138). I return to the matter of purposeful existence momentarily, on the topic of utility.

LICENSE TO IMPOSE PENAL HARM

The license in this case is the power to judge, contain, and kill people. The license to harm offenders has both procedural and moral dimensions. Agents of the criminal justice system stress procedural license, which makes sense since they are charged with the duty of imposing penal harm. Judges in particular determine for the rest of us the conditions that add up to the license to perpetrate penal harm. In death penalty cases *Penry v. Johnson, Ring v. Arizona, Panetti v. Quarterman,* and *Smith v. Texas,* the U.S. Supreme Court justices concluded that conditions had not been met for proper imposition of the death penalty.[9] Their decisions highlight proper computations that add up to the harm of execution, or not. The *Smith v. Texas* court, for example, determined that "Smith is entitled to relief under the state harmless-error framework." The *Panetti v. Quarterman* justices "find the state court failed to provide the procedures to which petitioner was entitled under the Constitution; and . . . determine that the federal appellate court employed an improperly restrictive test when it considered petitioner's claim on incompetency on the merits."[10] In offering these measured judgments, the justices in effect approve of executions in other cases. In contrast, the ordinary citizens that we interviewed affirmed a moral rather than procedural license to do penal harm. A moral license to do penal harm is built largely on the retributive principle, according to which offenders deserve it because of the harm they have caused victims. Speakers' surrogates are entitled to mete such harm out.

Desert and Desire

Eighteeen of the thirty research participants, and all but one of those who supported the death penalty, spoke favorably of retribution.

INTERVIEWER: [Do you] think some [criminals] could be . . . rehabilitated?

EARL: No, I don't worry about that. That's . . . I don't . . . I don't know about that either. No, not if they've taken it

that far that they're in there for life. Now, they shoulda
thought about that before they made the decisions that put
'em in there.

Earl's immediate response that he doesn't "worry about" the
possibility of rehabilitation is interesting. It suggests that he
actively rejects an alternative to penal harm, as well as any moral
disquiet over such harm. Another bold illustration of a quest to
harm came from death penalty *opponents* who supported penal
harm through imprisonment. They saw prison as giving offenders more of what they deserve:

> I say keep 'em locked *up,* but don't *kill* 'em, because . . . if
> you do that [incarceration], um, they're actually being *more*
> punished. (Gabriella)

> I don't think it's violent enough in some cases. Ya know,
> just puttin' somebody to death. Ya know, according to
> what their crime was, it's an easy way out for me. (Michelle)

These speakers took for granted that offenders should be
made to feel pain. A few research participants said that they
would favor harsh punishment and especially execution if a
loved one of theirs were harmed. As discussed previously, such
a rationale undermines the macrocosmic triumph of penal harm,
turning it into a microcosmic, or personal, project (Campbell
1949). Some would call this revenge rather than retribution
because it makes central victims' desire for payback.

> How would I feel, if someone did this to my parents, blah
> blah blah? And that's when I think capital punishment would
> be . . . would suffice, and would, ya know, be acceptable.
> Um, and again, I'm not saying that it's right, but I wouldn't
> be . . . it wouldn't be a problem. I can put it like that. (Jeff)

> And then for people who've just committed crimes that are
> just *so* awful, they may not ever do it again but . . . how can

you justify to the families of the victims that this person is out on the streets and they have the opportunity to commit another crime? Even if they never would. (Ali)

Jeff's remarks suggest that revenge is itself not "right" but that it inspires acceptable punishment nonetheless. Philosophers explain the connection. According to Jeffrie Murphy, the moral license to punish is ultimately about honoring victims. The would-be harm agent takes crime to be a signifier: "One reason we so deeply resent moral injuries done to us is not simply that they hurt us in some tangible or sensible way; it is because such injuries are also messages—symbolic communications. They are ways a wrongdoer has of saying to us, 'I count but you do not,' 'I can use you for my purposes,' or 'I am here up high and you are there down below'" (1988, 25). Murphy conceptualizes retribution as a symbolic gesture to deny the offender's false claim of superiority to the victim. Jean Hampton concurs that "punishment is uniquely suited to the vindication of the victim's relative worth" (1988, 128). The harm is done to communicate that the victim should not have been debased. The logic finds expression in the naming of crime-fighting laws after victims, such as Megan's Law.

Murphy's and Hampton's take on punishment as victim-centered runs up against the hegemonic legal discourse, in Western societies, according to which the offender has violated the state by violating the state's law. Nor does their perspective readily explain the sizable percentages of people punished in the United States for violating drug laws, as these individuals have harmed no specific victim. Regardless, the rhetoric of penal harm in the name of individual victims is potent. "It is as though all of us are victims," Todd Clear explains (1994, 119). We license ourselves to do penal harm nominally out of respect for victims, however substantively real the victim or the victimization.

Whereas the victim was overpowered in the criminal event, the penal harm agent is strong. The agent has defeated the offender on the victim's behalf and is fully justified in deploying the power to punish. Dan McAdams's argument that Americans narrate themselves as a chosen people, a "redeemer nation" (2006, 104), might explain the strength of the license we in the United States give to the state to punish to the utmost. McAdams observes, "The redemptive self is not a violent story, *but it is a story that can be read as one that might conceivably condone aggression in the name of redemption.* . . . In order to redeem the world, the chosen people must fight the holy war. They must defeat the forces of evil and chaos" (255–257; emphasis in original). Richard Slotkin (1973) notes the American myth of "regeneration through violence"—the title of his classic book.

In the American story of punishment, "The world consists mainly of victims and victimizers" (Kay 2005, 3) and never the twain shall meet. Therefore, it is not surprising that convicts rarely qualify as victims, although we know them to have sustained plenty of injury before and after criminal justice involvement. Imprisonment regularly does harm above and beyond that which it is designed to do, as when prisoners are assaulted, raped, or killed by other prisoners and correctional officers. Even the wrongly convicted have trouble obtaining recognition (let alone compensation) for the harm done to them unjustifiably. When confronted with structural injustices in the name of penal harm, both the Supreme Court justices and the individuals we interviewed denied the power to address them or else underestimated how deeply embedded in systems they are. In *Porter v. Nussle,* the problem of correctional officers' assaulting inmates was talked about, not as grounded in the penal harm enterprise generally, but rather as "a systemic problem traceable to poor hiring practices, inadequate training, or insufficient supervision."[11] The implication here is that the basic penal harm project is sound and that it minds its boundaries; *undue* harm is anomalous. The reader might at this point be reminded of speakers' construction of harm to nonhuman animals as unsystematic, any excesses stem from the irrational behavior of individuals. There is no license for such harm. In contrast, the system acts with good intentions.

Beyond prison walls, a great deal of victimization is not specified as such, and many victims remain silent concerning their victimization. They endure, or fear, blame and shame from family members, community members, and criminal justice agents. Steve, one of the individuals we interviewed, shared a painful story of being gang-raped by a group of boys at the age of thirteen.

INTERVIEWER: Okay, so all that you could remember was walking home and not saying anything. And . . . and then you were thinking . . .

STEVE: [*Sobbing.*] And I, uh, asked, well, there wasn't any question in my mind that I wasn't going to say anything. I knew it. I wasn't going to say anything, but I thought about the reasons why I wasn't going to say anything. Uh, something like this, you're supposed to have a family, and, uh, I knew that if I told my parents what had happened that my father would beat me, probably to an inch of my life, and I'd spend the rest of my life looking, having to see their looks, because they certainly would have looked at me differ . . . differently I know, for the rest of my life. And, so I didn't say anything. Not for thirteen to thirty-se . . . not for twenty-four years.

The story of penal harm casts victims as symbolic beneficiaries. Yet institutionally embedded cultural notions of crime, victims, and criminals—such as who the proper victim of rape is—constrain the story that gets told. The standard story does nothing to illuminate myriad neglected harms.

Just as only some people are proper victims, only some people are proper agents of penal harm. Generally speaking, penal harm is the province of white men. In a dominant, classic American story, the hero is a white man avenging the defilement of a white woman (Slotkin 1973). The state stands in for that heroic figure, who alone possesses the prerogative to inflict injury on the antihero.[12]

The Utility of Penal Harm

The principle of utility was by far the most frequently voiced license for penal harm in our interviews. A normative theory, utilitarianism states that moral decisions should be guided by the goal of maximizing human happiness (Shaw 1999). The utilitarian logic is consequentialist: the utilitarian weighs the costs and benefits of action in determining how to act. Susan shared the following take on the death penalty:

INTERVIEWER: Do you think that capital punishment is ever acceptable?
SUSAN: I really don't. I don't think that it's accomplishing anything.

Matt said he had "heard that it costs more to execute somebody than it does to keep them in prison the rest of their life," leading him to support life imprisonment because it would have "the least [negative] impact on the public." But Rose opposed imprisonment, saying, "I think it's ineffective and it makes the situation worse. And it's very expensive."

A common discourse related to utility had to do with offenders' presumably miniscule contribution to the larger society, previously discussed in terms of reduction. Ali remarked, "If a person can no longer be a functioning part of society, then I don't really see the point of keeping them around and wasting all of the money and resources on them." Ali assumes the indirect power to determine whether others live or die, and they are allowed to live only insofar as they have a function or purpose.

Earl was vehement in his utility-based support for the death penalty:

> They're not anything of any value to the country. Or the nation or our . . . or mankind. When they're in there for doing somethin' that are proven . . . that they were *proven* that they done something without a doubt. I don't have any use for the people myself. I think they should be ejected. I mean *injected*. And just get rid of 'em. Why . . . why feed 'em and put up with 'em? We got enough people that are *worthy* of feeding without feeding them . . . people that's been convicted. *Convicted* now. Totally. Life in prison, three life sentences: give me a break! G-get 'em *out* of here. Just move 'em out.

Like the penal harm enterprise generally, Earl reduces people to their use-value. Not coincidentally, the logic of people's usefulness also supports slavery and capitalism, harm enterprises with historically strong relationships to criminal punishment. This logic is played out in our system of plea bargaining: the more information one has to offer the state, the less penal harm one can usually expect to sustain. Injected or otherwise socially "ejected" (to use Earl's slip of the tongue), the individual is removed from a society where only the "worthy" may live. These schemes for gaining use-value from people conjure agents within their rights—an authority on moral grounds. We saw in chapter 4 that meat eaters similarly situate themselves as authorized by utilitarian considerations; in contrast, genocidal agents described utility as *driving* genocide (chapter 3), thus channeling a logic of powerlessness.

THE NECESSITY OF PENAL HARM

In our research interviews, penal harm, and imprisonment in particular, was presumed to be a social necessity. Some speakers deemed penal harm to be crucial without further qualification.

INTERVIEWER: What do you think about incarceration?
THERESA: It's totally necessary.
INTERVIEWER: What do you think about incarceration?
CHARLES: Um, as in?
INTERVIEWER: As in putting people in jail or prison. Like, how do you feel about it?
CHARLES: Just putting people in jail?
INTERVIEWER: Yeah.
CHARLES: Okay, um, I think it's absolutely necessary, um, obviously.

The necessity of imprisonment is "obvious" to Charles. More often, and when pressed to elaborate, speakers laid out the need for penal harm by discussing the target's threat to the rest of us. The target of penal harm is a *perpetual* hazard. Theresa conveyed this sense of being ever-threatened by serious offenders, hence the inevitability of the death penalty:

INTERVIEWER: What is your opinion about the death penalty?
THERESA: That's a really hard one [*sigh*]. Um. Unfortunately, there are some people that, as a society we just really can't handle them and their behavior, and the death penalty is just our last option. So I'm not against it. I feel that it's a valid form that we do have to go to that point in some . . . with some people.

Given the danger posed by (some) offenders, no alternative exists save to harm them. Patty said, "I think that if you do something wrong, and I leave you out here, you're gonna do it again." Critical of imprisonment and other criminal justice policies, Jane nonetheless allowed, "It's one of those acceptable harms that you might have to [do]." Although necessity is not absolute in her formulation, it is conceivable: necessity could ultimately guide one's actions. For some the need for prisons is regrettable, while others are bolder in their endorsement.

The common theme is that imprisonment is not a freely chosen policy.

Future danger is the main driver of penal harm policy in the United States. The deterrence and incapacitation doctrines rationalize punishment based on the threat posed by offenders, including would-be offenders who might be influenced by general deterrence. Note that policies of general deterrence reflect a particular process of reduction, where the current offender is made into a vehicle for preventing crime by other people.

MIXED MESSAGES

We arrive again at a power paradox. To assert a need to act in a particular way and to assert one's license to do so are two rather different things. The one conjures a powerless actor, the other a powerful one. Yet within the same statement, speakers combined the logics of powerlessness or necessity with the license to do penal harm.

INTERVIEWER: What is your attitude toward [the death penalty]?

GEORGE: I think there are some . . . instances where . . . it . . . it's the only thing to do. Um. Superegregious people just need to be vanished from the earth. Like . . . Jeffrey Dahmer. There was no reason for him to go to prison. He got . . . he got killed in prison, but . . . ya know. Ya know there are some people that are so . . . heinous, that . . . the only *punishment* . . . and it's . . . it's not a . . . I don't think it's a deterrent to future criminals. But it . . . some . . . some people . . . that's what you deserve. Sorry. It's just . . .

INTERVIEWER: So it's a desert thing.

GEORGE: It's . . . it's a retribution or . . . there's no reason to have that person on the planet anymore. It's harmful to society . . . it's more harmful to have that person on the planet than it is to kill them.

Reference to "the only thing to do" is at odds with that of retribution and deserts. The former conjures a powerless actor whose back is against the wall, the latter a powerful, choosy one.

Like lay speakers, members of the Supreme Court, the very highest court in the United States, both denied and asserted power. A rhetoric of compulsion is discernible in doctrinal statements, but so too is a message of agency and license, as in the *Ewing v. California* decision: "Throughout the States, legislatures enacting three strikes laws made a deliberate policy choice that individuals who have repeatedly engaged in serious or violent criminal behavior, and whose conduct has not been deterred by more conventional approaches to punishment, must be isolated from society in order to protect the public safety."[13] Note the paradox in that awkward formulation: Legislatures have chosen ("deliberate policy choice") a necessity ("must be isolated").

Supreme Court justices make regular appeals to precedent; indeed, their decisions read like analyses of what has been decided before. Besides precedent, the justices base their decisions on the U.S. Constitution and national opinion, on which state policies are said to rest. They alternately reference these as binding their hands and granting them power. In *Ewing v. California,* the justices declared, "We do not sit as a 'superlegislature' to second-guess these policy choices." Instead they deferred to the State of California, whose three-strikes law Gary Ewing had protested. Concluding statements in the case of *Kansas v. Marsh* are notable for the can't-do attitude they communicate:

> Because the criminal justice system does not operate perfectly, abolition of the death penalty is the only answer to the moral dilemma the dissent poses. This Court, however, does not sit as a moral authority. Our precedents do not

prohibit the States from authorizing the death penalty, even in our imperfect system. And those precedents do not empower this Court to chip away at the States' prerogatives to do so on the grounds the dissent invokes today.[14]

Elsewhere, though, the court clearly asserts its power. In *Kennedy v. Louisiana* the justices quoted their own remarks from *Coker v. Georgia:* "The Constitution contemplates that in the end our own judgment will be brought to bear on the question of the acceptability of the death penalty under the Eighth Amendment." They continue delicately to advance their powerful position as moral evaluators: "It must be acknowledged that there are moral grounds to question a rule barring capital punishment for a crime against an individual that did not result in death."[15] In addition, the court consistently endorses retribution by judging the rectitude of calculations of the proportionality of punishment. With their specifications, the court confirms the power to punish.

When "having to" take certain harmful action aligns with being licensed or licensing oneself to do so against a reduced target, the result is likely to be harm. In the present case, having to inflict penal harm derives from the perpetual threat of crime. The punisher is practical, not necessarily virtuous. In contrast, the retributive rationale associated with license does not merely legitimize harm: it casts it as good. The license to harm derives from the popular project of vanquishing the wrongdoer, who has sent an erroneous message of superiority to the symbolic victim by doing wrong, and who is not worth keeping alive and well. The story of penal harm is that the punisher-hero triumphs over the villainous and dangerous adversary. Through a license to achieve either a microcosmic or macrocosmic purpose, the hero is both empowered to do harm and bound to do it.

What of the political economy of criminal justice, which decades of critical criminologists have emphasized as shaping

the conduct of that system? A discursive engine keeps it running, and that same engine—the same set of meanings—keeps
other harmful practices running. My analysis brings those meanings to the surface. David Garland has recently set out a theoretical framework that considers punitive criminal justice in the
light of culture. He attributes the upward climb of incarceration
in the United States as well as England since the 1970s to a new
cultural enterprise of control: "This desire for security, orderli-
ness, and control, for the management of risk and the taming of
chance is, to be sure, an underlying theme in any culture. But in
Britain and America in recent decades that theme has become a
more dominant one, with immediate consequences for those
caught up in its repressive demands, and more diffuse, corrosive
effects for the rest of us" (2001, 194). We want to control
because we tell ourselves a tale of losing control—of being powerless in the face of menace—when we should rightly possess it.
The right to control and the ever-present threat of its disappearance are both especially salient in the American story. Livia
Polanyi observes that in this story, "proper people have power
over other people" (1985, 140). *Proper* people are people who
are entitled to wield power: the logic is circular. The structural
projects identified with mass incarceration, such as containing
minorities or the poor, rely on similar discourses concerning
power and powerlessness, as well as the simplified and down-
graded essence of the population in question.

CHAPTER 7

Synthesis

WHY WE HARM, the question that launched this book, is broad, some might say audaciously so. But I hope to have revealed the far greater audacity of the rhetoric of harm:

The circle of life constitutes some animals are bred to be nourishment (chapter 4).

I know you're not going to leave me, so I can crack you as much as I want (chapter 5).

When we spotted a small group of runaways trying to escape by creeping through the mud, we called them snakes (chapter 3).

We are not sufficiently alarmed by these discourses, least of all by those that concern conventional and everyday harm. I want to spotlight them, to launch a conversation about the role of discourse in harm doing. In this penultimate chapter I briefly synthesize the answer I have arrived at of why we harm. I also entertain some of the complexities of that answer, including potential problems, and recommend some research directions to locate resolutions to those problems.

We do harm because of cultural logics, typically in the form of stories, that reduce the target of harm and conjure ourselves as both authorized to harm and powerless not to. Observers of types of harmful action not examined in this book have arrived at similar theories. Consider the conclusion that Martha Huggins, Mika Haritos-Fatouros, and Philip Zimbardo reach based on their study of secret police engaged in torture: "We discovered that serial atrocity was nurtured out of an interrelated dynamic that included three spheres: the politics of an internal security ideology; the specialized hierarchy and competitive organization of social control units; and the associated social psychology of deindividuation, obedience, dehumanization, modeling violence's acceptability, and moral disengagement" (2002, 161–162). Thus, in their study, reduction (deindividuation, dehumanization), license (specialized hierarchy), and powerlessness (internal security ideology) are all in motion.

Oliver McTernan touches on storied powerlessness and license in describing the motivations of one Islamic man, who had spent most of his life in France, inspired to commit terrorist acts: "even though his rebellion against the society in which he was educated was triggered by a deep sense of grievance, it is his faith that provides the ideology that sustains him in the conviction that it is his task to change the world in accordance with the designs of God" (2003, 28). Grievance is one text, the designs of God another. What about the Westerners who, once presumably familiar, became this man's adversaries? They too are "made up."

A Reduced Target

The target of harm is my enemy, a Westerner, an inmate, a suspect, a terrorist, an Arab, an American, a communist, a savage, the prisoner, a faggot. She is a bitch, my wife, my woman, a cockroach, a nigger, a kike. Its flesh is "meat." He is just a kid. She is just a hooker. It is just a fly. It is prey. It is my property. Reduction might pay *too* much attention to targets, as with genocide and penal harm, where they are hyped as monsters, or render them invisible, as with the nonhumans we mistreat.

Reduction essentially entails obscuring the array of unique interests and experiences of the target.

The actor's interests may be cast in such a way that they overshadow those of the target. No discursive room is left for the intricacies of the target's experience. In answer to the interviewer's question of whether eating meat causes harm, research participants thought immediately of their own health interests, just as our dependence on meat has scholars most concerned with environmental strains and health problems that afflict humans. A more subtle version of this maneuver is a flattening identification such that the target is merely an adversary or potential adversary in one's story. Americans' depiction of Arabs, according to Edward Said, is illustrative:

> So far as the United States seems to be concerned, it is only a slight overstatement to say that Moslems and Arabs are essentially seen as either oil suppliers or potential terrorists. Very little of the detail, the human density, the passion of Arab-Moslem life has entered the awareness of even those people whose profession it is to report the Arab world. What we have instead is a series of crude, essentialized caricatures of the Islamic world presented in such a way as to make that world vulnerable to military aggression. (1980)

This kind of reduction involves not grasping—not even recognizing—most of what the Other has going on.

Reduction might allow the actor to deny that harm to the target is harm at all. This seems commonly to be the case with harm to nonhuman beings, including animals, plants, and the earth. Denial of harm is also found among sexual violators, who tell themselves and others that their victims enjoy the sexual contact. Consistent with Gresham Sykes and David Matza's (1957) notion of the denial of injury, our interviews revealed that target reduction may be captured in ready-made expressions and even single words such as "meat," whose ramifications the speaker is hardly aware of. That is to say, language plays a major role in such denial. The language with which our research participants described certain actions such as meat eating had stripped away suffering. Carol Cohn, who conducted participant-observation research with nuclear defense planners, reports on the planners' use of language to detach themselves from the harm it was their job to organize:

> Language that is abstract, sanitized, full of euphemisms; language that is sexy and fun to use; paradigms whose referent is weapons; imagery that domesticates and deflates the forces of mass destruction; imagery that reverses sentient and nonsentient matter, that conflates birth and death, destruction and creation—all of these are part of what makes it possible to be radically removed from the reality of what one is talking about and from the realities one is creating through the discourse. (1987, 715)

However radical their break from reality, Cohn shows that the nuclear scientists spoke in familiar ways. Their denial of harm was molded from collective constructions.

The case of domestic violence demonstrates that harm agents reduce even significant and beloved others. Reduction based on gender and age is commonly seen here: the construction of marked difference sets the terms for reduction of the target. Sometimes harm agents laud their targets. The exceptional minority artist often comes in for such treatment from whites. The hunter's prey may be honored as magnificent. And the victim of partner abuse may be put on a pedestal when not being beaten. The harm agents in question are honoring their targets for a certain limited number of qualities, consistent with reducing them.

THE ESSENTIAL PROTAGONIST

Generally speaking, to reduce a target is to allege that the target's complexity is less than one's own. We usually know ourselves as complex, as having multiple interests and projects. Yet very often we fail to grasp or to evoke the variety of what we too have going on. Rwandan Hutu killer Pancrace described this process: "The Hutu always suspects that some plans are cooking deep in the Tutsi character, nourished in secret since the passing of the ancien régime. He sees a threat lurking in even the feeblest or kindest Tutsi" (Hatzfeld 2003, 219). Pancrace reduces the enemy as well as his own group, the Hutus, for the latter are ever the would-be victims. Similarly, Adolf Hitler's deindividuation of Jewish people goes hand in hand with his deindividuation of Germans, as when he refers to "the striving of the Jewish people for world domination, a process which is just as natural as the urge of the Anglo-Saxon to seize domination of the earth" ([1925] 1999, 661). The essential German is the virtuous, brave, and nation-loving Aryan. Just as Paulo Freire's (1970) oppressors equate their own being with oppressing, harm agents come to narrow their existence and interests. In an extension of sociology's labeling theory, agents' reduction of others occurs prior to or at least concurrent with the reduction of selves.

Scholars reduce harm agents in their theoretical work on harm. Daniel Jonah Goldhagen's (1996) account of the Holocaust, emphasizing the so-called eliminationist anti-Semitism of virtually all Germans, has been much criticized in this regard. His argument—that Germans hated Jews and that they were universally possessed of a desire to exterminate Jews—drastically curtails our view of the interests of Germans as individuals. Mainstream criminology is often called out for a tendency toward reductionist perspectives on its subjects and especially on "offenders" (Woolford 2006). Dependent on government agencies for data on offenders and funding to support data collection and analysis, researchers tend to assume the point of view of the state, which, in the name of criminal justice, treats people and their lives as categories. I have used those categories (e.g., "offender") for the sake of clear exposition. In so doing

I reproduce the reductive tendencies of my cultural community. Yet social actors and researchers alike condense information about individuals: knowledge and the symbolic processes that aid knowledge are simply *that way*. Reduction may well be a normal aspect of social life. What I want to highlight is a reduction that goes beyond that which sustains the collective good.

POWER AND POWERLESSNESS

What I have termed a license to harm empowers the licensee to act in a particular way. Licenses are always signified into existence, although their foundations may be material. Therefore, actors get creative in claiming a license to harm. For example, a license may be conjured out of the presence of opportunities, the absence or weakness of sanctions, or the availability of the means to harm. In *Fist Stick Knife Gun* Geoffrey Canada (1995) argues that easy access to guns since the late 1970s enabled more fatal violence than had instruments previously available in poverty-stricken Harlem. Whereas weapons vary in their potential to do lethal harm, they are also texts that shape people's construction of powerful selves. Other such texts include job titles, principles, edicts, the word of God, and nature. The essence of the license to harm is the positive authority that it grants. Then there are claims of powerlessness, which include a variety of references to the actor's inability to act differently. The harm's inevitability, the atmosphere for harm, the agent's anger, and the demands of self-defense and survival more generally are among the logics of powerlessness that speakers summon.

Criminology is replete with realist accounts of crime committed by the impoverished, whose illegal action is some function of their dire circumstances. Having no or few alternatives but to sell drugs or rob seems to describe only some harm doers. Most of us have options, although they may be constrained. Moreover, in cases of environmental degradation through consumption, industrialized farming, imprisonment, and genocide, the actors, especially the planners, are powerful, at least relatively speaking. Still, these actors very often *profess* powerlessness: "there's no other way," "my hands are tied," and "desperate times call for desperate measures." Deeply impressed by the actors' agency, scholars see claims of powerlessness as excuses designed to mitigate sanctions, avoid shame, and maintain their relative privilege. Along these lines, Susan Faludi responds to unsympathetic treatment in her account of contemporary American men suffering a sense of powerlessness: "Many in the women's movement and in the mass media complain that men just 'don't want to give up the reins of power.' But that would seem to have little applicability to the situations of most men, who individually feel not the reins of power in their hands but its bit in their mouths" (1999, 41). Faludi's study of men in diverse sites—including football fan clubs, the militia movement, and the porn industry—reveals an "ever-prying, ever-invasive beam reducing men to objects," such as women have long suffered (599). Faludi thus validates men's claims of powerlessness.

Charles Tittle's general theory of deviance, control balance theory, is likewise centrally concerned with real power and real powerlessness. He proposes that deviance is likely when an individual exercises either too much or too little control; deviance in either case is an effort to gain greater control. For Tittle, control surpluses and control deficits are "social structural facts" (1995, 207). Yet in his 1995 book and in a 2004 revision of the theory, Tittle acknowledges that perception is consequential. "In view of [the] human tendency to perceive reality incorrectly, an individual's actual control ratio may sometimes be far less relevant than the control ratio he or she thinks is operating" (1995, 205). Appraising control balance theory, Joachim Savelsberg unpacks the experience of powerlessness:

First, constraints may not be experienced by individuals as such. Our mental maps of our cities and neighborhoods, for example, are selective. They leave out what we do not know. Or, power in the sense of hegemonic power, or structural power may not be noticeable to individuals exposed to it. Second, individuals may be aware of such power and the limitations it imposes on them, but power may be legitimized in their belief systems. Formal organizations only function because decision making is differentiated and because authority structures are in place. We may not appreciate every decision to which we are exposed. We may experience some decisions as constraints. But we may also perceive them as legitimate. Third, individuals may even benefit from constraints. (1999, 336)

Savelsberg's insight, that our awareness and understanding of subjection is likely to be incomplete, also applies to our awareness and understanding of the power at our disposal. We may discount our power, either cynically or because that is the way things really look to us.

Likewise, researchers of white-collar crime allow that even "truly" powerful actors may experience a call to hold onto power or secure more of it as a compulsion. Neal Shover and Andy Hochstetler consider the ways in which a choice made by an elite offender is experienced as *no* choice. The need to stay competitive is potentially "all-consuming" (2006, 64). Individuals facing financial problems arrive at "what they experience as a breaking point" (114). "Under pressure to offend, resigning from the organization most always is an option, but it may not seem that way" (119).

Psychological theories of crime posit powerlessness in part as a psychic condition, with its earliest source in one's family of origin. David Gadd and Tony Jefferson see trouble where a predisposition thus formed meets gender expectations. Regarding intimate partner violence, they observe that "many of the feelings experienced by violent men are themselves a product of the tensions between their own psychological sense of powerlessness and more widely endorsed expectations about masculinity and femininity" (2007, 146). The idea that violence is a function of "entitlement thwarted" (Kimmel 2011, 385) built on public conceptions of masculine privilege is incomplete, however. A more in-depth cultural reading shows that it is also associated with a story of (incipient) loss of control, one's back to the wall, so to speak. I also question the idea that powerlessness is necessarily loathsome to men. As James Gilligan states, "The most dangerous men on earth are those who are afraid that they are wimps" (1997, 66). Men (and women) regularly channel logics of vulnerability. We claim to be governed by any number of things—the tumult of the moment, one's own hand, a need for meat protein, the command of a higher-up, the color of fury, the steady din of danger. The rhetorics of powerlessness are at our disposal: we access them without fear and often without much thought or awareness.

A POWER PARADOX

For most scholars in this field, power and powerlessness seem to volley from two sides of a net dividing the real and structural from the constructed and cultural. Structurally powerful actors point to made-up constraints while structurally powerless actors strive pathetically to aggrandize themselves. Instead, I endorse a view of both power and powerlessness as discursively formed regardless of the speaker's real social position.

Harm agents project both power and powerlessness: I am empowered to engage in a particular harmful action *and* that action has a life of its own. Other theorists have noted the power paradox, though not in those terms. Jack Katz offers the best example I know of in criminology. In *Seductions of Crime* he considers a variety of offenders for whom the criminal act—truly an act—promises to help actors to know themselves or to be known in a certain way. The outcome of the dramatization is always essentially uncertain. Concerning armed robbers, for example, Katz states, "In addition to the suspense that arises from the inevitable unknowns about the reactions of victims and co-offenders, the offender is in suspense most profoundly about himself," as he does not know exactly what he will do (1988, 192). The offender's perception of the criminal act as potentially addictive or overwhelming—out of his control—is precisely what makes it so alluring. In all cases, Katz observes, "the participants are playing with the line between the sense of themselves as subject and object, between being in and out of control, between directing and being directed by the dynamics of the situation" (8). Hence, critiquing both positivist and materialist accounts of crime, Katz contends that "the causes of crime are constructed by the offenders themselves, but the causes they construct are lures and pressures that they experience as independently moving them toward crime" (216). Offenders actively contribute to that which compels them. Just as reduction of others is a normal process for making sense of the world, the power paradox is akin to the normal human tension between creativity and constraint. Social actors and scholars alike grapple with that tension, asking whether people have agency or are mainly directed by structure. The power paradox behind harm is a radical, discursive expression of the human condition.

How does the power paradox motivate? I am speculating here; there are several possibilities.

- The harm resolves the paradox. The actor's rightful authority is regained.
- The paradox stirs us emotionally. It induces anxiety in the batterer, frenetic excitement in the genocidaire, righteous indignation in the punisher.
- The paradox all but guarantees the action, as we are both released and entitled to it. For the meat eater, it acts like a narcotic, providing a cozy emotional berth.

Because some harms entail passion while others are carried out with little affect, even for the same type of action—consider

impassioned mobs and steely bureaucrats in a single massacre—
harm clearly does not *require* emotion.

Over and beyond its potential to motivate, the power
paradox is a material-cum-ideological engine for harm by
organizations, granting permission on the one hand while earn-
ing sympathy on the other. For example, a gas-drilling company
appeals to its legal right to utilize a damaging technique and the
practical necessity of that technique. Starting inquiry with stories and minimizing the role of emotions permit us to say something about multiple levels of participation in harm using the
same theoretical tools. Both individuals and collectives, including corporations and other organizations, identify themselves
and are identified by others; both pursue action based on stories
of who they are and who others are.

What Is Said and What Is Not Said

Storytelling, like communication generally, excludes a great
deal of experience to make a point. In other words, what is *not*
said communicates: as Peter Berger and Thomas Luckmann
observe, "the greater part of reality-maintenance in conversation is implicit, not explicit. Most conversation does not in so
many words define the nature of the world. Rather, it takes
place against the background of a world that is silently taken for
granted" (1966, 152). What we take for granted speaks volumes,
in fact. For example, the logic equating meat eating and survival
need not be stated. The more presumptive speakers take such
understandings to be, the less likely they are to be formally
explicated or interrogated in speech. In that case speakers
merely hint at that logic. So it was that, often, our research participants seemed irritated by interviewers' close questioning of
the ideological foundations of harm.

Of course, much goes unspoken because we lack the information to inform speech, and often we lack the information

because we avoid the information. Many of those we interviewed proclaimed ignorance about harms in which they were
implicated, including harms associated with meat processing,
conduct toward prisoners, and other corporate and government
policies. The knowledge of these harms could disturb us (Case
et al. 2005). Or, we may avoid information about large-scale
action because we tell ourselves there is nothing we could do
about it anyway (Fenster 2006). In this formulation, a logic of
powerlessness precedes information avoidance. But the relationship could conceivably run the other way as well. Not knowing
maintains the claim that one is incapable of resisting.

SAYING AND DOING

All manner of acts in the world could be considered
antecedents to the discourses that instigate harm. I do not mean
to vanquish other factors, only to expose the way stories coop-
erate with them. Among these factors are harmful actions themselves. Cultural criminologists and constitutive criminologists,
each with a distinct conceptual vocabulary, aptly note that
harmful action itself tells a story about who the harm agent is.
Sociological perspectives on gender performance suggest the
same (Butler 1990; Messerschmidt 1993, 1997, 2000; West and
Zimmerman 1987). For example, James Messerschmidt argues
convincingly that race, class, and gender identities are realized
through criminal behavior. He calls crime "a resource for doing
masculinity, race, and class [which] changes over time and is sit-
uated in specific social contexts" (1997, 64). Something similar
can be said of our "doing" of species and national identities. By
killing nonhuman animals, we disrupt our connection to them
and align ourselves with reasoning, rationality, and nonobjectiv-
ity (Bataille 1989). Genocidal violence effects reduction, as Liisa
Malkki puts it: "Through violence, bodies of individual persons
become metamorphosed into *specimens* of the ethnic category
for which they are supposed to stand" (1995, 88; emphasis in

original). In these cases, the harm is its own message about self vis-à-vis Other. The fact that harm is being done may signal license and thus embolden onlookers-cum-perpetrators. Therefore, we must speak differently to act differently, *and* we must act differently to speak differently. But how? How else could we speak? How else could we act? These are the concerns of the next and final chapter.

CHAPTER 8

Unmaking Misery

I know he had unusual eyes,
Whose power no orders could determine.
Not to mistake the men he saw,
As others did, for gods or vermin.

—Thom Gunn

If you believe that you can damage, then
believe that you can fix. If you believe that
you can harm, then believe that you can heal.

—Rebbe Nachman of Breslov

WE NEED A kinder way of living and inter-
acting with one another. Where shall we start? This chapter
outlines some ideas for unmaking misery, following the analysis
laid out in the book so far and connecting where relevant to
other perspectives.

TELL TRUE STORIES

My thesis has been that certain stories engender misery.
They motivate and legitimize harmful action. Therefore, storytelling per se is most assuredly not the solution to the problem
of harm, as some would romanticize. But neither should storytelling be seen as the problem. After all, we humans rely on
stories to make meaning. This book itself tells a story in which
the understanding of a problem, gained in the first seven chapters, gives way to redemption in this coda.

We should tell *true* stories. Stories are not true by virtue of faithfulness to some preinterpreted world, since they always occupy "the domain midway between the real and the imaginary" (Bruner 1990, 55). By true stories I mean ones whose complexity approximates the complexity of lived experience. True stories integrate all one's own feelings and ideas, all the allegiances and anchors of selfhood. They nod toward past, present, and future. The characters in true stories are ever on their way to becoming something else. This is the case—it is at least hinted at—even when the storyteller pronounces the story's end. For the sake of unmaking misery, it is particularly important that storytellers acknowledge the dynamism of living. We have seen that target reduction freezes who the target—and often too the speaker—is. True stories suggest variable personifications, readings, twists, and endings. We also saw the dangers in claiming both power and powerlessness. True stories feature more authentic appraisals of one's capacities and incapacities.

It is as important to listen to such stories as it is to tell them. In this age of rapid-fire, often-canned ("LOL!") communication, true stories may seem anachronistic. They are likely to be lengthy and unfamiliar, as storytellers weave together strands of experience and feeling in creative ways. It takes a bit more time to digest them. The exchange of new, true stories demands patience.

Correctional and other forms of treatment would seem to be logical sites for moving stories toward greater truth, as they are efforts to promote change and often use talk as a means to do so. Instead of top-down treatment protocols where practitioners instruct clients on their erroneous thoughts and methods of reasoning (Fox 1999), I have in mind a discussion-oriented protocol and a sociological curriculum that interrogates harm-promoting discourses. Treatment programs for convicted offenders should "encourage participants to become cultural critics, appraising the story forms they have adopted" (Presser

2008, 155). Such programs have radical promise because they invite penal subjects to speak and they focus on such speech as opposed to static and solitary proclivities. In addition, the rehabilitative goal of a "good life" (Ward and Maruna 2007) reflects a truer story than the one that offenders are usually encouraged to tell, of "changing their ways." The former gets real about the fact that "offenders" are like "us" and want what the rest of us want—to live happily, meaningfully, and without suffering. The latter—the status quo—tends to reduce people to problems.

Yet, however modeled, corrections-based change does not go nearly far enough for my vision of harm reduction. Correctional programs deal with a minute sector of the harm-causing population. It is a sector whose harms have been overstated relative to other harms; the latter include indirect varieties instigated by planners and tolerated by the rest of us. As seen in chapter 6, drawing a distinction between correctional clients and the rest of us feeds the rhetoric of penal harm. So we need general forums where our harmful actions and arrangements are made perfectly clear, their underlying logics are interrogated, the connections between logics and harms are discerned, and feasible plans are made for change. Such forums might be sponsored by mass media or academia and convened in civic spaces such as online and face-to-face social groups. As in correctional settings, participants would generate "replacement discourses," which Stuart Henry and Dragan Milovanovic characterize as "a non-reificatory connecting of the way we speak with our social relations and institutions" (1996, 219). As groups deliberate on social problems, they would monitor their stories for reduction of self and Other and for power paradoxes.

RESTORE JUSTICE

Stuart Henry and Dragan Milovanovic turn to restorative justice for replacing harmful discourses "without using counter-power/force" (1996, 220). The restorative justice philosophy attends to harm and defines justice as repair of harm. In the context of criminal justice, a restorative justice practice asks "Who has been harmed?" and "What do they need?" The paradigmatic restorative justice practice involves meetings of victims and offenders. Circles in North America and family group conferences in Australia and New Zealand convene such meetings, where questions are asked and answered and stories are exchanged. Participants typically sit in a circle and pass a token, a stick or a stone, that permits its holder to speak uninterrupted. (This use of sticks and stones is a neat reversal of their figurative purpose to hurt.) On the possibilities of discursive change through restorative justice storytelling, John Braithwaite notes,

> In restorative justice conferences, after each individual has [his or her] stories listened to, new stories that allow new identities are coauthored by a plurality of stakeholders in the injustice. . . . The coauthorship produces a narrative in many voices, each appropriating and transforming the others in ways unlikely to be akin to simple morality tales offered to children. Rather, the circle's story is likely not to have clear villains and heroes. (2006, 428–429)

In other words, restorative justice can encourage the telling of true stories, where the message surfaces that we all play a part in harm. Another potential message of restorative justice encounters is that none of us wishes to harm per se. Both of these messages can unsettle notions of who we and others are. In addition, some would wed restorative justice programs to other models of peaceful exchange, such as nonviolent communication, where we understand our experiences and the experiences of others in terms of feelings and needs (D. Sullivan 2007). This type of communication shakes up reductions and power paradoxes because it provides a new vocabulary for talking about identity and agency.

Restorative justice is oriented to both discourse and action. In addition to storytelling, the restorative justice philosophy emphasizes accountability—an active sort with specific requirements:

> This means that (the offender) must be encouraged to develop as complete an understanding as possible of what he has done (i.e., what his actions have meant to the other person involved, and to acknowledge his role in it). He must also be allowed and encouraged to make things right to the extent that it is possible to do so. And he should participate in finding ways that this can be done. (Zehr 1995, 43)

Claims of powerlessness are actively countered in the ideal restorative justice encounter. According to Robert Yazzie and James Zion, peacemaking circles challenge "the 'we can't do anything' excuse" (2003, 146). A story of power is renewed, but it is a story of the power to do good. Harms are addressed concretely, nurtured by a logic of collective capacity for problem solving.

Restorative justice must be used faithfully, in line with its core philosophy, and more broadly if it is to make much of an impact in countering harm. Currently, it is oriented toward conflict and crime intervention, responding to hurts already inflicted. As such, many restorative justice programs tend to operate from categories and logics inherited from criminal justice agencies (Presser and Hamilton 2006). I envision restorative justice as a method of communication where received constructions of lived experience and future choices are held up to scrutiny. I imagine restorative justice circles taking place in many institutions, workplaces, and organizations, simply as a way of conducting meetings.

Social divisions set limits, intentionally ("Children should be seen and not heard") and unintentionally, on the stories that one can tell and that others hear (Frank 2010). Restorative justice circles should question these limits, not perpetuate them

(Presser and Hamilton 2006). For those of us in the socially constructed global, national, ethnic, zoological, and moral center, it is often difficult to entertain what and who is forgotten. Therefore, we must think hard about those whose vantage points are not getting expressed and work to get them expressed for the sake of social justice. This effort will be not be unproblematic, as exemplified by debates over abortion, where spokespersons for and against claim to advocate for one whose voice is not being heard—fetus or pregnant woman. Social scientific research findings, ethical reasoning, and a critical vantage must be brought to bear.

Dispel the Myth of Closure

A great deal of harm is rationalized as redress for prior harm done to us. The harm promises to balance the ledger and thus to end our suffering. We should dispel the implied "myth of closure" (Madeira 2012), the myth that "as soon as the offender has been successfully blamed and purposefully harmed, the cycle is complete" (Clear 1994, 141) and the "score is even" (Hampton 1988, 128). We should circulate instead the idea that "action has no end" (Arendt 1958, 233). For Madeira, the question of how we can act less harmfully is one of how we should grieve after we have been harmed. She expands the concept of closure so that it "becomes an immeasurably broader term that comports with individual and cultural instincts to work through trauma and 'become' survivors, to endure not only the traumatic event but also the trauma of reconstruction" (2012, xxiv). We need consciousness raising that questions the notion that a second harm is an element of reconstruction.

The project of reconstruction involves deciding how to remember what happened to us. Lori Amy cites literary theorist Tzvetan Todorov on the distinction between literal and exemplary memory:

> Literal memory is self-referential. In this way of remembering, we rehearse, over and over, the litany of wrongs done

to us. We are the innocent victims who suffer, whose suffering nobody else can imagine, and we suffer from the actions of a guilty perpetrator, the evil other. Literal memory is static, stuck, and its repetition of this history of suffering reentrenches pain, anger, hatred. . . . In contrast, exemplary memory connects us to the suffering of others and to the world around us. In this way of remembering, we see that all events have a history, a context, a trajectory into the future. We see human beings as being like us. (2010, 160)

The connection between the two sorts of memory and reduction of targets is clear. When we understand that all events have a "trajectory into the future," we are led to consider the consequences of whatever actions we are considering because we understand that stories keep getting told and continue informing action.

LICENSE OURSELVES TO DO GOOD

Shadd Maruna found that persons who desisted from property offending narrated claims that they were "very much in control of their current and future life direction" (2001, 13). These ex-offenders were also highly likely to speak of giving back: they deployed redemption scripts. We might say that they conjured a new license to do good. To do so on a mass scale we must be bold in the face of large-scale, pervasive, and popular harms. We must reject tales of futility. We must also integrate into our stories responsibility for the well-being of others.

The business of doing good is dangerous territory, and I don't want to minimize that. One person's good is another's evil. Many known harm agents, including history's notorious leaders of genocide, conjure themselves as helpers. As Plato put it, "Every soul pursues the good and does whatever it does for its sake" (1955, 505e). Collective storytelling, promoted by restorative justice principles and practices where disparate interests are discussed, is the hedge I have in mind against narrow definitions of the good.

STUDY HARM

We should all study harms. The proliferation of crises in the modern day both promote and reflect increased use of rhetorics of powerlessness, leading to increased harm. Whereas Steven Pinker (2011) observes that violence has decreased, I contend that *harm* has not. There is reason to believe, for example, that the beating of children has decreased worldwide over the past several centuries, whereas degradation of the atmosphere has increased.

By studying harm we nudge the academy in at least three important directions. First, we expand horizons from the usual victims, such as humans. Second, we unsettle existing hierarchies according to which intended and direct harms are more serious than unintended and indirect harms, because harm, not law, occupies center stage. Third, we gain awareness of researchers' contributions to harmful patterns. The dominant scientific method takes beings out of context, leading, as Sandra Harding notes, to "the simultaneous de-development and continual re-creation of 'others.'" Harding specifies targets of such "othering"—"third world peoples, women, the poor, nature" (1991, ix)—but the objects of academic reification are in fact much broader. We should recontextualize those we study, which will mean qualitative research projects that devote greater attention to "the means by which subjects make sense of discursive strategies and the way in which these hermeneutic fibres feed into the warp and weft of everyday life" (Mythen and Walklate 2006, 393). It is easier to observe what harm agents are like and to collect *the* attitudes that they hold than it is to clarify how they articulate a *variety* of attitudes as they make meaning in the different moments of their lives.

TAKE ACTION

The project of reducing harm in the world is daunting and not just because of its ubiquity. Our constructions of self and Other feel natural, authentic, and inevitable. To see the world any differently requires "unusual eyes" (Gunn 1969)—a sociological imagination. It might be easier to begin to unmake misery by changing action than by changing discourse. As we have seen, harmful practices and cultural signification are mutually constitutive. Harm results from the logics; harm also fortifies the logics. For example, zoos evolve from reduction of targets and effect such reductions (Jamieson 2006, 142). We could abolish zoos as we know them, which would ultimately effect a change in how we talk about the animals we keep there now. The availability of guns, drug and alcohol addiction, and gross economic inequalities nationally and globally support contradictory claims of powerfulness and powerlessness and lead us to reduce ourselves and others. So, after all, at the end of this leg of the journey through the cultural bases of harmful actions, I urge intervention into their material bases. A change in some part of a harmful enterprise as an initial intervention can be a means to more radical transformation.

Notes

1. I do not address harms by nonhuman animals, which I venture requires a different theoretical approach. The analysis also excludes acts of nature (e.g., fatal lightning strikes) where human activity is, arguably, not implicated.

2. Cultural and other social forces influence which harms cause us concern and which actions we even call harms (see Butler 2004). The labeling of an action as harm is a socially contingent process (S. Cohen [1972] 2002; Loseke 2003). Whereas I grant victims privileged status as classifiers of harm, the process whereby they do the classifying is always socially mediated and problematic.

3. However, where victims lack or are denied the capacity to express their suffering, this approach may not yield justice. I return to this serious issue in the concluding chapter of the book.

4. Wieviorka (2009, chap. 3) observes that the call for a study of harm has as its context the decline of the nation-state. If this view is correct, the plea of critical criminologists to move beyond the study of state-designated harms has in effect been answered by historical events.

5. As Beccaria put it, "The true measure of crimes is . . . the harm done to society" ([1764] 1963, 64).

6. Friedrichs and Schwartz (2007) consider the practical, academic implications of trading criminology for zemiology, such as dim prospects for funding and being taken seriously.

7. I use the female pronoun when referring to the harm agent as a purposive alternative to male-centric language, except in chapter 5 on intimate partner violence. There I use the male pronoun, given the predominance of men among batterers.

8. I exclude from "unreflective harms" those of which the actor has no knowledge. Admittedly, a fine line divides harming unknowingly and harming unreflectively.

9. Furthermore, I know of no study of boys' torture of nonhuman animals "for fun," although anecdotal evidence suggests that it is pervasive.

10. Neisser (2002) problematizes the reduction of persons to "targets" in wartime. I use the term target more generally, to mean the being who is harmed.

11. I use the terms "narratives" and "story" interchangeably, although the distinctions that some scholars make are compelling and useful. Some observe, for example, that one's "personal" story draws on broader cultural narratives (see Frank 2010, 14).

CHAPTER 2 WE ARE WRITTEN: A NARRATIVE FRAMEWORK OF HARM

1. See for example Bruner (1990), Gergen and Gergen (1988), Kerby (1991), Linde (1993), O'Connor (2000), Polkinghorne (1988), Ricoeur (1984, 1985), Sarbin (1986), Schiffrin (1996), Somers (1994), and Wood and Rennie (1994).

CHAPTER 3 GENOCIDE, HARM OF HARMS

1. In 1948 the United Nations defined genocide as "any of the following acts committed with intent to destroy, in whole or in part, a national, ethnical, racial or religious group, as such: killing members of the group; causing serious bodily or mental harm to members of the group; deliberately inflicting on the group conditions of life, calculated to bring about its physical destruction in whole or in part; imposing measures intended to prevent births within the group; [and] forcibly transferring children of the group to another group" (United Nations 1948).
2. Sampson, Raudenbush and Earls (1997) propose that residents of neighborhoods who perceive themselves as collectively capable to solving collective problems prevent crime. Residents' perceptions, and not collective efficacy as would-be offenders construct it, are related to crime.
3. See, for example, Alvarez (1997); Browning (1993); Fox and Levin (1998); Freire (1970); Huggins, Haritos-Fatouros, and Zimbardo (2002); Kelman (1973); Scheper-Hughes and Bourgois (2004); and Young (2003).
4. Hatzfeld provides only first names of the Rwandan killers.
5. "Like wolves they flung themselves in packs of eight or ten again and again on their enemies, and little by little actually began to thrash them [opponents of his National Socialist German Workers' Party] out of the hall" (Hitler [1925] 1999, 505).

CHAPTER 4 INSTITUTIONALIZED HARM THROUGH MEAT EATING

1. These thirty interviews supplement the thirty used to study penal harm (see chapter 6).
2. Research participants are referred to by assigned pseudonyms.

CHAPTER 5 INTIMATE PARTNER VIOLENCE:
A FAMILIAR STRANGER

1. The ten countries in the sample were Bangladesh, Brazil, Ethiopia, Japan, Namibia, Peru, Samoa, Serbia and Montenegro, Thailand, and the United Republic of Tanzania.
2. A constructionist approach to power and powerlessness is consistent with the phenomenon of battering by persons of apparent privilege.
3. Renzetti (1992) studied IPV among lesbians; Cruz and Firestone (1998) among gay men. In these two studies abusers and victims were of the same sex.
4. Two articles—Hydén and McCarthy (1994) and Hydén (1995)—reported on the same research, although the 1994 article discussed additional research (on incest) and the articles reported some different statements by the same sample of informants.
5. In some studies, including Hearn's (1998) and Ptacek's (1988), it is unclear whether the same or different men are quoted.

CHAPTER 6 PENAL HARM: STIGMA,
THREAT, AND RETRIBUTION

1. Although our small sample is not a secure basis for determining rates, it should be noted that the sample is relatively well educated, and education is positively correlated with opposition to the death penalty.
2. *LaRoyce Lathair Smith v. Texas*, 550 U.S. 297 (2007); *Larry Begay v. United States*, 553 U.S. 137 (2008).
3. *Patrick O. Kennedy v. State of Louisiana*, 554 U.S. 407 (2008), at 27–28; *Erlich Anthony Coker v. State of Georgia*, 433 U.S. 584 (1977).
4. *Ralph Baze and Thomas C. Bowling v. John D. Rees*, 553 U.S. 35 (2008), at 12.
5. *Daryl Renard Atkins v. Virginia*, 536 U.S. 304 (2002), at 6; *Kansas v. Michael Lee Marsh II*, 548 U.S. 163 (2006), at 16.
6. *Johnny Paul Penry v. Gary L. Johnson*, 532 U.S. 782 (2001), at 18, 13; *Roper v. Simmons*, 543 U.S. 551 (2005).
7. *Begay*, 553 U.S.; *Gary Ewing v. State of California*, 538 U.S. 11 (2003).
8. *Roper*, 543 U.S. at 20.
9. *Penry*, 532 U.S.; *Timothy Stuart Ring v. Arizona*, 536 U.S. 584 (2002); *Scott Louis Panetti v. Nathaniel Quarterman*, 551 U.S. 930 (2007); *Smith*, 550 U.S.
10. *Smith*, 550 U.S. at 18; *Panetti*, 552 U.S. at 2.
11. *Correction Officer Porter et al. v. Ronald Nussle*, 534 U.S. 516 (2002), at 12.
12. We saw this chivalrous license in the context of intimate partner violence as well.
13. *Ewing*, 538 U.S. at 12.
14. *Id.* at 15; *Kansas*, 548 U.S. at 17.
15. *Coker* 433 U.S.; *Kennedy*, 554 U.S. at 24.

References

Abraham, Margaret. 1999. "Sexual Abuse in South Asian Immigrant Marriages." *Violence against Women* 5 (6): 591–618.

Adams, Carol J. 1994. *The Sexual Politics of Meat: A Feminist-Vegetarian Critical Theory*. New York: Continuum.

AFSC (American Friends Service Committee). 2012. "Solitary Confinement Facts." http://afsc.org/resource/solitary-confinement-facts.

Agnew, Robert. 1992. "Foundation for a General Strain Theory of Crime and Delinquency." *Criminology* 30:47–87.

———. 2010. "A General Strain Theory of Terrorism." *Theoretical Criminology* 14 (2): 131–153.

———. 2011. *Toward a Unified Criminology: Integrating Assumptions about Crime, People, and Society*. New York: NYU Press.

Alexander, Michelle. 2010. *The New Jim Crow: Mass Incarceration in the Age of Colorblindedness*. New York: New Press.

Alvarez, Alexander. 1997. "Adjusting to Genocide: The Techniques of Neutralization and the Holocaust." *Social Science History* 21 (2): 139–178.

Amy, Lori E. 2010. *The Wars We Inherit: Military Life, Gender Violence, and Memory*. Philadelphia: Temple University Press.

Anderson, Elijah. 1999. *Code of the Street: Decency, Violence, and the Moral Life of the Inner City*. New York: Norton.

Anderson, Kristin L., and Debra Umberson. 2001. "Gendering Violence: Masculinity and Power in Men's Accounts of Domestic Violence." *Gender and Society* 15 (3): 350–380.

Arendt, Hannah. 1958. *The Human Condition*. Chicago: University of Chicago Press.

———. 1963. *Eichmann in Jerusalem: A Report on the Banality of Evil*. New York: Viking.

———. 1969. *On Violence*. Orlando, FL: Harcourt, Brace.

Arluke, Arnold. 2002. "A Sociology of Sociological Animal Studies." *Society and Animals* 10 (4): 369–374.

Bandura, Albert. 1973. *Aggression: A Social Learning Analysis*. Englewood Cliffs, NJ: Prentice-Hall.

———. 1990. "Mechanisms of Moral Disengagement." In *Origins of Terrorism: Psychologies, Ideologies, Theologies, States of Mind*, edited by Walter Reich, 161–191. New York: Cambridge University Press.

Barthes, Roland. 1977. "Introduction to the Structural Analysis of Narratives." In *Image, Music, Text*, 79–124. Translated by Stephen Heath. New York: Hill and Wang.

Bataille, Georges. 1989. *Theory of Religion*. New York: Zone Books.

Beah, Ishmael. 2007. *A Long Way Gone: Memoirs of a Boy Soldier*. New York: Farrar, Straus, and Giroux.

Beccaria, Cesare. (1764) 1963. *Of Crimes and Punishments*. Translated by Henry Paolucci. Indianapolis, IN: Bobbs-Merrill. Citations refer to the 1963 edition.

Becker, Howard S. 1963. *Outsiders: Studies in the Sociology of Deviance*. New York: Free Press.

Beirne, Piers. 2009. *Confronting Animal Abuse*. Lanham, MD: Rowman and Littlefield.

Bélanger-Vincent, Ariane. 2009. "Discourses That Make Torture Possible: The Abu Ghraib Case." *Explorations in Anthropology* 9 (1): 36–46.

Beneke, Timothy. 1982. *Men on Rape*. New York: St. Martin's Press.

Bergen, Raquel Kennedy. 1995. "Surviving Wife Rape: How Women Define and Cope with the Violence." *Violence against Women* 1 (2): 117–138.

Berger, Peter L., and Thomas Luckmann. 1966. *The Social Construction of Reality: A Treatise in the Sociology of Knowledge*. New York: Anchor.

Black, Donald. 1983. "Crime as Social Control." *American Sociological Review* 48:34–45.

Booker, Vaughan. 1994. *From Prison to Pulpit: My Road to Redemption*. With David Phillips. New York: Cadell and Davies.

Boswell, A. Ayres, and Joan Z. Spade. 1996. "Fraternities and Collegiate Rape Culture: Why Are Some Fraternities More Dangerous Places for Women?" *Gender and Society* 10:133–147.

Bourgois, Philippe. 2003. *In Search of Respect*. 2nd ed. Cambridge: Cambridge University Press.

Box, Steven. 1983. *Power, Crime, and Mystification*. New York: Tavistock.

Braithwaite, John. 2006. "Narrative and 'Compulsory Compassion.'" *Law and Social Inquiry* 31 (2): 425–446.

Browne, Angela. 1987. *When Battered Women Kill*. New York: Free Press.

Browning, Christopher R. 1993. *Ordinary Men: Reserve Police Battalion 101 and the Final Solution in Poland*. New York: HarperCollins.

Bruner, Jerome. 1990. *Acts of Meaning*. Cambridge, MA: Harvard University Press.

Bui, Hoan N. 2002. "Immigration Context of Wife Abuse: A Case of Vietnamese Immigrants in the United States." In *It's a Crime: Women and Justice,* edited by Roslyn Muraskin, 394–410. Englewood Cliffs, NJ: Prentice Hall.

———. 2004. *In the Adopted Land: Abused Immigrant Women and the Criminal Justice System.* Westport, CT: Praeger.

Burbank, Victoria K. 1992. "Fight! Fight! Men, Women, and Interpersonal Aggression in an Australian Aboriginal Community." In Counts, Brown, and Campbell 1992, 33–42.

Butler, Judith. 1990. *Gender Trouble: Feminism and the Subversion of Identity.* New York: Routledge.

———. 2004. *Precarious Life: The Powers of Mourning and Violence.* London: Verso.

Campbell, Joseph. 1949. *The Hero with a Thousand Faces.* New York: Pantheon.

Canada, Geoffrey. 1995. *Fist Stick Knife Gun: A Personal History of Violence in America.* Boston: Beacon.

Carson, E. Ann, and William J. Sabol. 2012. *Prisoners in 2011.* Washington, DC: Bureau of Justice Statistics, U.S. Department of Justice. http://bjs.ojp.usdoj.gov/content/pub/pdf/p11.pdf.

Case, Donald O., James E. Andrews, J. David Johnson, and Suzanne L. Allard. 2005. "Avoiding versus Seeking: The Relationship of Information Seeking to Avoidance, Blunting, Coping, Dissonance, and Related Concepts." *Journal of the Medical Library Association* 93 (3): 353–362.

Chancer, Lynn S. 1992. *Sadomasochism in Everyday Life: The Dynamics of Power and Powerlessness.* New Brunswick, NJ: Rutgers University Press.

Clear, Todd R. 1994. *Harm in American Penology: Offenders, Victims, and Their Communities.* Albany: State University of New York Press.

Cohen, Lawrence E., and Marcus Felson. 1979. "Social Change and Crime Rate Trends: A Routine Activities Approach." *American Sociological Review* 44 (August): 588–608.

Cohen, Stanley. (1972) 2002. *Folk Devils and Moral Panics.* 3rd ed. London: Routledge. Citations refer to the 2002 edition.

———. 2001. *States of Denial: Knowing about Atrocities and Suffering.* Cambridge: Polity.

Cohn, Carol. 1987. "Sex and Death in the Rational World of Defense Intellectuals." *Signs: Journal of Women in Culture and Society* 12 (4): 687–718.

Coleman, James William. 1987. "Toward an Integrated Theory of White-Collar Crime." *American Journal of Sociology* 93 (2): 406–439.

Collier, Paul. 2000. "Doing Well Out of War: An Economic Perspective." In *Greed and Grievance: Economic Agendas in Civil Wars,* edited by Mats Berdal and David M. Malone, 91–111. Boulder, CO: Lynne Rienner.

Connell, R. W. 1995. *Masculinities*. Berkeley: University of California Press.

Cruz, J. Michael, and Juanita M. Firestone. 1998. "Exploring Violence and Abuse in Gay Male Relationships." *Violence and Victims* 13 (2): 159–173.

Cullen, Francis T., Bonnie S. Fisher, and Brandon K. Applegate. 2000. "Public Opinion about Punishment and Corrections." *Crime and Justice* 27:1–79.

Das Dasgupta, Shamita, and Sujata Warrier. 1996. "In the Footsteps of 'Arundhati.'" *Violence against Women* 2 (3): 238–259.

Day, L. Edward, and Margaret Vandiver. 2000. "Criminology and Genocide Studies: Notes on What Might Have Been and What Still Could Be." *Crime, Law, and Social Change* 34:43–59.

DeKeseredy, Walter S. 2011. *Violence against Women: Myths, Facts, Controversies*. Toronto: University of Toronto Press.

Dobash, Rebecca Emerson, and Russell Dobash. 1979. *Violence against Wives: A Case against the Patriarchy*. New York: Free Press.

Dobash, Russell P., R. Emerson Dobash, Margo Wilson, and Martin Daly. 1992. "The Myth of Sexual Symmetry in Marital Violence." *Social Problems* 39 (1): 71–91.

Dollard, John, Leonard W. Doob, Neal E. Miller, Orval Hobart Mowrer, and Robert R. Sears. 1939. *Frustration and Aggression*. New Haven, CT: Yale University Press.

Douglas, Mary. 1986. *How Institutions Think*. Syracuse, NY: Syracuse University Press.

DPIC (Death Penalty Information Center). 2012a. "Executions by Year." http://www.deathpenaltyinfo.org/executions-year.

———. 2012b. "National Polls and Studies." http://www.deathpenalty info.org/national-polls-and-studies.

Draper, Patricia. 1992. "Room to Maneuver: !Kung Women Cope with Men." In Counts, Brown, and Campbell 1992, 43–61.

Eisikovits, Zvi. 1996. "The Aftermath of Wife Beating: Strategies of Bounding Violent Events." *Journal of Interpersonal Violence* 11 (4): 459–474.

Elliot, Pam. 1996. "Introduction: Shattering Illusions: Same-Sex Domestic Violence." *Journal of Gay and Lesbian Social Services* 4 (1): 1–8.

Fairclough, Norman. 1992. *Discourse and Social Change*. Cambridge: Polity.

Faludi, Susan. 1999. *Stiffed: The Betrayal of the American Man*. New York: HarperCollins.

FBI (Federal Bureau of Investigation). 2012. "Expanded Homicide Data." Table 10. *Crime in the United States, 2010*. Washington, DC: FBI. http://www.fbi.gov/about-us/cjis/ucr/crime-in-the-u.s/2010/crime-in-the-u.s.-2010/tables/10shrtb110.xls.

Feldman, Allen. 1991. *Formations of Violence: The Narrative of the Body and Political Terror in Northern Ireland.* Chicago: University of Chicago Press.

Fenster, Mark. 2006. "The Opacity of Transparency." *Iowa Law Review* 91:885–949.

Fernandez, Marilyn. 1997. "Domestic Violence by Extended Family Members in India: Interplay of Gender and Generation." *Journal of Interpersonal Violence* 12 (3): 433–455.

Festinger, Leon. 1957. *A Theory of Cognitive Dissonance.* Stanford, CA: Stanford University Press.

Flynn, Dan. 2012. "Five States Now Have 'Ag-Gag' Laws on the Books." *Food Safety News,* March 26. http://www.foodsafetynews.com/2012/03/five-states-now-have-ag-gag-laws-on-the-books/.

Foer, Jonathan Safran. 2009. *Eating Animals.* New York: Little, Brown.

Fox, James A., and Jack Levin. 1998. "Multiple Homicide: Patterns of Serial and Mass Murder." *Crime and Justice: A Review of Research* 23:407–455.

Fox, Kathryn J. 1999. "Changing Violent Minds: Discursive Correction and Resistance in the Cognitive Treatment of Violent Offenders in Prison." *Social Problems* 46:88–103.

Frank, Arthur W. 2010. *Letting Stories Breathe: A Socio-Narratology.* Chicago: University of Chicago Press.

Freire, Paulo. 1970. *Pedagogy of the Oppressed.* New York: Herder and Herder.

Friedrichs, David O., and Martin D. Schwartz. 2007. "Editors' Introduction: On Social Harm and a Twenty-First Century Criminology." *Crime, Law, and Social Change* 48 (1–2): 1–7.

Gadd, David. 2000. "Masculinities, Violence and Defended Psychosocial Subjects." *Theoretical Criminology* 4 (4): 429–449.

Gadd, David, and Tony Jefferson. 2007. *Psychosocial Criminology: An Introduction.* Los Angeles: Sage.

Gagné, Patricia L. 1992. "Appalachian Women: Violence and Social Control." *Journal of Contemporary Ethnography* 20 (4): 387–415.

Gamson, William A. 1995. "Hiroshima, the Holocaust, and the Politics of Exclusion." *American Sociological Review* 60 (1): 1–20.

Garcia-Moreno, Claudia, Henrica A.F.M. Jansen, Mary Ellsberg, Lori Heise, and Charlotte H. Watts. 2006. "Prevalence of Intimate Partner Violence: Findings from the WHO Multi-Country Study on Women's Health and Domestic Violence." *Lancet* 368 (9543): 1260–1269.

Garland, David. 1990. *Punishment and Modern Society: A Study in Social Theory.* Chicago: University of Chicago Press.

———. 2001. *The Culture of Control: Crime and Social Order in Contemporary Society.* Chicago: University of Chicago Press.

Georgesen, John, and Monica J. Harris. 1998. "Why's My Boss Always Holding Me Down? A Meta-Analysis of Power Effects on Performance Evaluation." *Personality and Social Psychology Review* 2:184–195.

Gergen, Kenneth J., and Mary M. Gergen. 1988. "Narrative and the Self as Relationship." In *Advances in Experimental Social Psychology*, edited by Leonard Berkowitz, 21:17–56. San Diego, CA: Academic Press.

Gilbert, Louisa, Nabila El-Bassel, Valli Rajah, Anthony Foleno, and Victoria Frye. 2001. "Linking Drug-Related Activities with Experiences of Partner Violence: A Focus Group Study of Women in Methadone Treatment." *Violence and Victims* 16 (5): 517–536.

Gilligan, Carol. 1982. *In a Different Voice: Psychological Theory and Women's Development.* Cambridge, MA: Harvard University Press.

Gilligan, James. 1997. *Violence: Reflections on a National Epidemic.* New York: Vintage Books.

Girard, René. 1977. *Violence and the Sacred.* Baltimore: Johns Hopkins University Press.

Glaze, Lauren E., and Erika Parks. 2012. *Correctional Populations in the United States, 2011.* Washington, DC: Bureau of Justice Statistics, U.S. Department of Justice.

Goldhagen, Daniel Jonah. 1996. *Hitler's Willing Executioners: Ordinary Germans and the Holocaust.* New York: Vintage.

Gopnik, Adam. 2012. "The Caging of America." *The New Yorker*, January 30. http://www.newyorker.com/arts/critics/atlarge/2012/01/30/120130crat_atlarge_gopnik.

Gottfredson, Michael R., and Travis Hirschi. 1990. *A General Theory of Crime.* Stanford, CA: Stanford University Press.

Guerino, Paul, Paige M. Harrison, and William J. Sabol. 2011. "Prisoners in 2010." Bureau of Justice Statistics, U.S. Department of Justice. http://bjs.ojp.usdoj.gov/content/pub/pdf/p10.pdf.

Gunn, Thomas. 1969. "Epitaph for Anton Schmidt." In *Selected Poems, 1950–1975,* by Thom Gunn, 64–65. New York: Farrar, Straus, and Giroux.

Hagan, John, and Wenona Rymond-Richmond. 2009. *Darfur and the Crime of Genocide.* New York: Cambridge University Press.

Hamilton, Malcolm. 2006. "Eating Death: Vegetarians, Meat and Violence." *Food, Culture, and Society: An International Journal of Multidisciplinary Research* 9 (2): 155–177.

Hampton, Jean. 1988. "The Retributive Idea." In *Forgiveness and Mercy,* by Jeffrie G. Murphy and Jean Hampton, 111–161. Cambridge: Cambridge University Press.

Harding, Sandra. 1991. *Whose Science? Whose Knowledge? Thinking from Women's Lives.* Ithaca, NY: Cornell University Press.

Hattery, Angela J. 2009. *Intimate Partner Violence.* Lanham, MD: Rowman and Littlefield.

Hatzfeld, Jean. 2003. *Machete Season: The Killers in Rwanda Speak.* New York: Picador.

Hearn, Jeff. 1998. *The Violences of Men: How Men Talk About and How Agencies Respond to Men's Violence to Women.* London: Sage.

Hegland, Mary Elaine. 1992. "Wife Abuse and the Political System: A Middle Eastern Case Study." In Counts, Brown, and Campbell 1992, 203–218.

Henry, Stuart, and Dragan Milovanovic. 1996. *Constitutive Criminology: Beyond Postmodernism.* London: Sage.

Hiebert, Maureen S. 2008. "The Three 'Switches' of Identity Construction in Genocide: The Nazi Final Solution and the Cambodian Killing Fields." *Genocide Studies and Prevention* 3 (1): 5–29.

Hil, Richard, and Rob Robertson. 2003. "What Sort of Future for Critical Criminology?" *Crime, Law, and Social Change* 39 (1): 91–115.

Hillyard, Paddy, Christina Pantazis, Steve Tombs, and Dave Gordon, eds. 2004. *Beyond Criminology: Taking Harm Seriously.* London: Pluto.

Hitler, Adolf. (1925) 1999. *Mein Kampf.* Translated by Ralph Manheim. Boston: Houghton Mifflin.

Huggins, Martha K., Mika Haritos-Fatouros, and Philip G. Zimbardo. 2002. *Violence Workers: Police Torturers and Murderers Reconstruct Brazilian Atrocities.* Berkeley: University of California Press.

Hughes, Everett C. 1945. "Dilemmas and Contradictions of Status." *American Journal of Sociology* 50 (5): 353–359.

Hydén, Margareta. 1995. "Verbal Aggression as Prehistory of Woman Battering." *Journal of Family Violence* 10 (1): 55–71.

Hydén, Margareta, and Imelda Colgan McCarthy. 1994. "Woman Battering and Father-Daughter Incest Disclosure: Discourses of Denial and Acknowledgment." *Discourse and Society* 5 (4): 543–565.

ICPS (International Centre for Prison Studies). 2012. "World Prison Brief." http://www.prisonstudies.org/info/worldbrief/wpb_stats.php?area=all &category=wb_poprate.

Icyitegetse, Drocella. 2000. "Transcript." April 30, 1994. Montreal Institute for Genocide and Human Rights Studies (MIGS). http://migs.concordia.ca/links/documents/RR_30Apr94_eng_K023 –8739-K023–8758.pdf.

Jackson-Jacobs, Curtis. 2004. "Taking a Beating: The Narrative Gratifications of Fighting as an Underdog." In *Cultural Criminology Unleashed,* edited by Jeff Ferrell, Keith Hayward, Wayne Morrison, and Mike Presdee, 231–244. London: Glasshouse.

Jacoby, Russell. 2011. *Bloodlust: On the Roots of Violence from Cain and Abel to the Present.* New York: Free Press.

Jamieson, Dale. 2006. "Against Zoos." In *In Defense of Animals: The Second Wave,* edited by Peter Singer, 132–143. Malden, MA: Blackwell.

Jenkins, Richard. 2008. *Social Identity*. 2nd ed. London: Routledge.

Jones, Rachel K. 1993. "Female Victim Perceptions of the Causes of Male Spouse Abuse." *Sociological Inquiry* 63 (3): 351–361.

Justice Policy Institute. 2000. *The Punishing Decade: Prison and Jail Estimates at the Millennium*. Washington, DC: Justice Policy Institute. http://www.justicepolicy.org/images/upload/00–05_rep_punishing decade_ac.pdf.

Kambanda, Jean. 1994. "Transcript." April 12, 2002. Montreal Institute for Genocide and Human Rights Studies (MIGS). http://migs .concordia.ca/links/documents/RR_1May94_eng_K036–4107–K036–4129.pdf.

Kantengwa, Marie-France. 1999. "Transcript." June 9, 1994. Montreal Institute for Genocide and Human Rights Studies (MIGS). http://migs.concordia.ca/links/documents/RR_9Jun94_eng_K026 –1334-K026–1361.pdf.

Katz, Jack. 1988. *Seductions of Crime: The Moral and Sensual Attractions of Doing Evil*. New York: Basic Books.

Katz, Jackson. 2006. *The Macho Paradox: Why Some Men Hurt Women and How All Men Can Help*. Naperville, IL: Sourcebooks.

Kay, Judith W. 2005. *Murdering Myths: The Story behind the Death Penalty*. Lanham, MD: Rowman and Littlefield.

Kelman, Herbert C. 1973. "Violence without Moral Restraint: Reflections on the Dehumanization of Victims and Victimizers." *Journal of Social Issues* 29 (4): 25–61.

Kerby, Anthony Paul. 1991. *Narrative and the Self*. Bloomington: Indiana University Press.

Kimmel, Michael. 2011. *The Gendered Society*. 4th ed. New York: Oxford University Press.

Kipnis, David. (1972) 2006. "Does Power Corrupt?" In *Small Groups: Key Readings,* edited by John M. Levine and Richard L. Moreland, 177–186. New York: Psychology Press.

Kramer, Ronald C. 1985. "Defining the Concept of Crime: A Humanistic Perspective." *Journal of Sociology and Social Welfare* 12:469–487.

Labov, William, and Joshua Waletzky. 1967. "Narrative Analysis: Oral Versions of Personal Experience." In *Essays on the Verbal and Visual Arts,* edited by June Helms, 12–44. Seattle: University of Washington Press.

Langer, Lawrence L. 1997. "The Alarmed Vision: Social Suffering and Holocaust Atrocity." In *Social Suffering,* edited by Arthur Kleinman, Veena Das, and Margaret Lock, 47–65. Berkeley: University of California Press.

Langford, David R. 1998. "Social Chaos and Danger as Context of Battered Women's Lives." *Journal of Family Nursing* 4 (2): 167–181.

Lateef, Shireen. 1992. "Wife Abuse among Indo-Fijians." In Counts, Brown, and Campbell 1992, 185–201.

Le Bon, Gustav. 1903. *The Crowd: A Study of the Popular Mind*. London: Fisher Unwin.

Levinas, Emmanuel. 1985. *Ethics and Infinity: Conversations with Phillip Nemo*. Translated by Richard A. Cohen. Pittsburgh: Duquesne University Press.

Lewis, Ruth, Rebecca E. Dobash, Russell P. Dobash, and Kate Cavanagh. 2000. "Protection, Prevention, Rehabilitation or Justice? Women's Use of the Law to Challenge Domestic Violence." *International Review of Victimology* 7:170–205.

Linde, Charlotte. 1993. *Life Stories: The Creation of Coherence*. New York: Oxford University Press.

Lombroso, Cesare. 1876. *L'Uomo Delinquente* [Criminal Man]. Milan: Hoepli.

Loseke, Donileen R. 2003. *Thinking about Social Problems: An Introduction to Constructionist Perspectives*. 2nd ed. New York: Gruyter.

Lyng, Stephen. 2004. "Crime, Edgework and Corporeal Transaction." *Theoretical Criminology* 8 (3): 359–375.

Madeira, Jody. 2012. *Killing McVeigh: The Death Penalty and the Myth of Closure*. New York: NYU Press.

Magdol, Lynn, Terrie E. Moffitt, Avshalom Caspi, and Phil A. Silva. 1998. *Journal of Marriage and Family* 60 (1): 41–55.

Malkki, Liisa H. 1995. *Purity and Exile: Violence, Memory, and National Cosmology among Hutu Refugees in Tanzania*. Chicago: University of Chicago Press.

Maruna, Shadd. 2001. *Making Good: How Ex-convicts Reform and Rebuild Their Lives*. Washington, DC: American Psychological Association.

Mason, Carol. 2002. *Killing for Life: The Apocalyptic Narrative of Pro-life Politics*. Ithaca, NY: Cornell University Press.

Matza, David. 1964. *Delinquency and Drift*. New York: Wiley.

Matza, David, and Gresham M. Sykes. 1961. "Juvenile Delinquency and Subterranean Values." *American Sociological Review* 26 (5): 712–719.

Maynes, Mary Jo, Jennifer L. Pierce, and Barbara Laslett. 2008. *Telling Stories: The Use of Personal Narratives in the Social Sciences and History*. Ithaca, NY: Cornell University Press.

McAdams, Dan P. 2006. *The Redemptive Self: Stories Americans Live By*. New York: Oxford University Press.

McKee, Lauris. 1999. "Men's Rights/Women's Wrongs: Domestic Violence in Ecuador." In *To Have and to Hit: Cultural Perspectives on Wife Beating*, edited by Dorothy Ayers Counts, Judith K. Brown, and Jacquelyn C. Campbell, 168–186. Urbana: University of Illinois Press.

McTernan, Oliver. 2003. *Violence in God's Name: Religion in an Age of Conflict*. Maryknoll, NY: Orbis.

Mehrotra, Meeta. 1999. "The Social Construction of Wife Abuse: Experiences of Asian Indian Women in the United States." *Violence against Women* 5 (6): 619–640.

Messerschmidt, James W. 1993. *Masculinities and Crime: Critique and Reconceptualization of Theory.* Lanham, MD: Rowman and Littlefield.

———. 1997. *Crime as Structured Action: Gender, Race, Class, and Crime in the Making.* Thousand Oaks, CA: Sage.

———. 2000. *Nine Lives: Adolescent Masculinities, the Body, and Violence.* Boulder, CO: Westview.

Messinger, Adam M. 2011. "Invisible Victims: Same-Sex IPV in the National Violence Against Women Survey." *Journal of Interpersonal Violence* 26 (11): 2228–2243.

Michalowski, Raymond J. 1985. *Order, Law, and Crime: An Introduction to Criminology.* New York: Random House.

Michalski, Joseph H. 2004. "Making Sociological Sense Out of Trends in Intimate Partner Violence: The Social Structure of Violence against Women." *Violence against Women* 10 (6): 652–675.

Miller, Jody. 2008. *Getting Played: African American Girls, Urban Inequality, and Gendered Violence.* New York: NYU Press.

Mitchell, William E. 1992. "Why Wape Men Don't Beat Their Wives: Constraints toward Domestic Tranquility in a New Guinea Society." In Counts, Brown, and Campbell 1992, 89–98.

Morash, Merry, Hoan N. Bui, and Anna M. Santiago. 2000. "Cultural-Specific Gender Ideology and Wife Abuse in Mexican-Descent Families." *International Review of Victimology* 7:67–91.

Mukanyiligira, Josephine. 1999. "Transcript." June 1, 1994. Montreal Institute for Genocide and Human Rights Studies (MIGS). http://migs.concordia.ca/links/documents/RR_1Jun94_eng_K036 –4060-K036–4086.pdf.

Mullaney, Jamie L. 2007. "Telling It Like a Man: Masculinities and Battering Men's Accounts of Their Violence." *Men and Masculinities* 10 (2): 222–247.

Münkler, Herfried. 2005. *The New Wars.* Translated by Patrick Camiller. Cambridge: Polity.

Munro, Alice. 2009. "Too Much Happiness." In *Too Much Happiness: Stories,* 246–303. Toronto: McClelland and Stewart.

Murphy, Jeffrie G. 1988. "Forgiveness and Resentment." In *Forgiveness and Mercy,* by Jeffrie G. Murphy and Jean Hampton, 14–34. Cambridge: Cambridge University Press.

Mykoff, Moshe. 1996. *The Empty Chair: Finding Hope and Joy, Timeless Wisdom from a Hasidic Master, Rebbe Nachman of Breslov.* Woodstock, VT: Jewish Lights.

Mythen, Gabe, and Sandra Walklate. 2006. "Criminology and Terrorism: Which Thesis? Risk Society or Governmentality?" *British Journal of Criminology* 46:379–398.

Nager, Larry. 2002. "Jazz Fest's 40-Year Run Interrupted: Promoter to Try Again for 2003." *Cincinnati Enquirer*, April 10. http://www .enquirer.com/editions/2002/04/10/loc_jazz_fests_40-year.html.

Neisser, Phillip T. 2002. "Targets." In *Collateral Language: A User's Guide to America's New War*, edited by John Collins and Ross Glover, 138–153. New York: NYU Press.

Ni Aolain, Fionnuala D. 2009. "Exploring a Feminist Theory of Harm in the Context of Conflicted and Post-conflict Societies." Minnesota Legal Studies Research Paper 09–45 http://papers.ssrn.com/s013/ papers.cfm?abstract_id=1507793.

O'Connor, Patricia E. 2000. *Speaking of Crime: Narratives of Prisoners*. Lincoln: University of Nebraska Press.

Opotow, Susan. 1993. "Animals and the Scope of Justice." *Journal of Social Issues* 49 (1): 71–85.

Pemberton, Simon. 2007. "Social Harm Future(s): Exploring the Potential of the Social Harm Approach." *Crime, Law, and Social Change* 48:27–41.

Pew Center on the States. 2012. "Time Served: The High Cost, Low Return of Longer Prison Terms." http://www.pewstates.org/ uploadedfiles/PCS_Assets/2012/Pew_Time_Served_report.pdf.

Pinker, Steven. 2011. *The Better Angels of Our Nature: Why Violence Has Declined*. London: Penguin.

Plato. 1955. *The Republic*. London: Penguin.

Polanyi, Livia. 1985. *Telling the American Story: A Structural and Cultural Analysis of Conversational Storytelling*. Norwood, NJ: Ablex.

Polkinghorne, Donald E. 1988. *Narrative Knowing and the Human Sciences*. Albany: State University of New York Press.

Polletta, Francesca. 2006. *It Was Like a Fever: Storytelling and Protest in Politics*. Chicago: University of Chicago Press.

Presdee, Mike. 2000. *Cultural Criminology and the Carnival of Crime*. London: Routledge.

Presser, Lois. 2008. *Been a Heavy Life: Stories of Violent Men*. Urbana: University of Illinois Press.

———. 2009. "The Narratives of Offenders." *Theoretical Criminology* 13 (2): 177–200.

———. 2012. "Getting on Top through Mass Murder: Narrative, Metaphor, and Violence." *Crime Media Culture* 8 (1): 3–21.

Presser, Lois, and Cynthia A. Hamilton. 2006. "The Micro-Politics of Victim Offender Mediation." *Sociological Inquiry* 76 (3): 316–342.

Presser, Lois, and William V. Taylor. 2011. "An Auto-Ethnography of Hunting." *Crime, Law, and Social Change* 55 (5): 483–494.

Ptacek, James. 1988. "Why Do Men Batter Their Wives?" In *Feminist Perspectives on Wife Abuse*, edited by Kersti Yllo and Michele Louise Bograd, 133–157. Newbury Park, CA: Sage.

Purvin, Diane M. 2003. "Weaving a Tangled Safety Net: The Intergenerational Legacy of Domestic Violence and Poverty." *Violence against Women* 9 (10): 1263–1277.

Quinney, Richard, and John Wildeman. 1991. *The Problem of Crime: A Peace and Social Justice Perspective*. 3rd ed. London: Mayfield.

Radio Rwanda. 1994. "Transcript." May 24, 1994. Montreal Institute for Genocide and Human Rights Studies (MIGS). http://migs.concordia.ca/links/documents/RR_24May94_eng_K033_1902_K033_1949.pdf.

Rand, Michael R., and Linda E. Saltzman. 2003. "The Nature and Extent of Recurring Intimate Partner Violence against Women in the United States." *Journal of Comparative Family Studies* 34 (1): 137–149.

Reiman, Jeffrey, and Paul Leighton. 2010. *The Rich Get Richer and the Poor Get Prison: Ideology, Class, and Criminal Justice*. 9th ed. Boston: Allyn and Bacon.

Reitz, Ronda Redden. 1999. "Batterers' Experiences of Being Violent." In *Innovations in Feminist Psychological Research*, edited by Ellen B. Kimmel and Mary Crawford, 143–165. New York: Cambridge University Press.

Renzetti, Claire M. 1992. *Violent Betrayal: Partner Abuse in Lesbian Relationships*. Newbury Park, CA: Sage.

Ricoeur, Paul. 1984. *Time and Narrative*. Translated by Kathleen McLaughlin and David Pellauer. Chicago: University of Chicago Press.

———. 1985. "History as Narrative and Practice." Translated by Robert Lechner. *Philosophy Today* 29 (3–4): 213–222.

Riger, Stephanie, Sheela Raja, and Jennifer Camacho. 2002. "The Radiating Impact of Intimate Partner Violence." *Journal of Interpersonal Violence* 17 (2): 184–205.

Rosen, Karen H., and Kimberly Bird. 1996. "A Case of Woman Abuse: Gender Ideologies, Power Paradoxes, and Unresolved Conflict." *Violence against Women* 2 (3): 302–321.

Roy, Jody M. 2002. *Love to Hate: America's Obsession with Hatred and Violence*. New York: Columbia University Press.

Said, Edward W. 1980. "Islam through Western Eyes." *The Nation*, April 26. http://www.thenation.com/article/islam-through-western-eyes#.

Sampson, Robert J., Stephen W. Raudenbush, and Felton Earls. 1997. "Neighborhoods and Violent Crime: A Multilevel Study of Collective Efficacy." *Science* 277:918–924.

Sandberg, Sveinung. 2010. "What Can 'Lies' Tell Us about Life? Notes towards a Framework of Narrative Criminology." *Journal of Criminal Justice Education* 21 (4): 447–465.

———. 2013. "Are Self-Narratives Unified or Fragmented, Strategic or Determined? Reading Breivik's Manifesto in Light of Narrative Criminology." *Acta Sociologica* 56 (1): 65–79.

Sarat, Austin. 1993. "Speaking of Death: Narratives of Violence in Capital Trials." *Law and Society Review* 27 (1): 19–58.

Sarbin, Theodore R., ed. 1986. *Narrative Psychology: The Storied Nature of Human Conduct*. New York: Praeger.

Savelsberg, Joachim J. 1999. "Human Nature and Social Control in Complex Society: A Critique of Charles Tittle's Control Balance." *Theoretical Criminology* 3 (3): 331–338.

Schabas, William A. 2000. *Genocide in International Law: The Crime of Crimes*. Cambridge: Cambridge University Press.

Scheff, Thomas J. 1994. *Bloody Revenge: Emotions, Nationalism, and War*. Boulder, CO: Westview.

Scheper-Hughes, Nancy, and Philippe Bourgois. 2004. "Introduction: Making Sense of Violence." In *Violence in War and Peace,* edited by Nancy Scheper-Hughes and Philippe Bourgois, 1–33. Malden, MA: Blackwell.

Schiffrin, Deborah. 1996. "Narrative as Self-Portrait: Sociolinguistic Constructions of Identity." *Language in Society* 25 (2): 167–203.

Schwendinger, Herman, and Julia Schwendinger. 1970. "Defenders of Order or Guardians of Human Rights?" *Issues in Criminology* 5 (2): 123–157.

Scott, Marvin B., and Stanford M. Lyman. 1968. "Accounts." *American Sociological Review* 33 (1): 46–62.

Seu, Irene Bruna. 2010. "'Doing Denial': Audience Reaction to Human Rights Appeals." *Discourse and Society* 21 (4): 438–457.

Shaw, William H. 1999. *Contemporary Ethics: Taking Account of Utilitarianism*. Malden, MA: Blackwell.

Shill Schrager, Laura, and James F. Short Jr. 1980. "How Serious a Crime? Perceptions of Organizational and Common Crimes." In *White-Collar Crime: Theory and Research,* edited by Gilbert Geis and Ezra Stotland, 14–31. Thousand Oaks, CA: Sage.

Short, Lynn M., Pamela M. McMahon, Doryn Davis Chervin, Gene A. Shelley, Nicole Lezin, Kira Sue Sloop, and Nicola Dawkins. 2000. "A Case Study of Community-Based Responses to Rural Woman Battering." *Violence against Women* 8 (7): 845–872.

Shover, Neal, and Andy Hochstetler. 2006. *Choosing White-Collar Crime*. New York: Cambridge University Press.

Siegel, Lalenya Weintraub. 1995. "The Marital Rape Exemption: Evolution to Extinction." *Cleveland State Law Review* 43 (351): 351–378.

Silver, Daniel. 2011. "The Moodiness of Action." *Sociological Theory* 29 (3): 199–222.

Simmel, Georg. 1971. *On Individuality and Social Forms: Selected Writings*. Edited by Donald N. Levine. Chicago: University of Chicago Press.

Singer, Mark. 2002. "A Year of Trouble: A City Subverts Itself." *New Yorker,* May 20. http://www.newyorker.com/archive/2002/05/20/020520fa_FACT.

Singer, Peter. 2006. Introduction to *In Defense of Animals: The Second Wave*, edited by Peter Singer, 1–10. Malden, MA: Blackwell.

Slotkin, Richard. 1973. *Regeneration through Violence: The Mythology of the American Frontier, 1600–1860*. Norman: University of Oklahoma Press.

Smith, Philip. 1997. "Civil Society and Violence: Narrative Forms and the Regulation of Social Conflict." In *The Web of Violence: From Interpersonal to Global*, edited by Jennifer E. Turpin and Lester R. Kurtz, 91–116. Urbana: University of Illinois Press.

———. 2005. *Why War? The Cultural Logic of Iraq, the Gulf War, and Suez*. Chicago: University of Chicago Press.

Somers, Margaret R. 1994. "The Narrative Constitution of Identity: A Relational and Network Approach." *Theory and Society* 23:605–649.

Stanford, Craig B., and Henry T. Bunn, eds. 2001. *Meat-Eating and Human Evolution*. New York: Oxford University Press.

Sternberg, Robert J. 2003. "A Duplex Theory of Hate: Development and Application to Terrorism, Massacres, and Genocide." *Review of General Psychology* 7 (3): 299–328.

Stibbe, Arran. 2001. "Language, Power and the Social Construction of Animals." *Society and Animals* 9 (2): 145–161.

Stone, Albert. 1982. *Autobiographical Occasions and Original Acts*. Philadelphia: University of Pennsylvania Press.

Suicide Food. 2011. Accessed March 3, 2013. http://suicidefood.blogspot.com/.

Sullivan, Dennis. 2007. "Nonviolence Begins with Speech: An Interview with Emily Gaarder on the Practice of Nonviolent Communication." *Contemporary Justice Review* 10 (1): 131–142.

Sullivan, Dennis, and Larry Tifft. 2005. *Restorative Justice: Healing the Foundations of Our Everyday Lives*. 2nd ed. Monsey, NY: Willow Tree.

Sykes, Gresham M., and David Matza. 1957. "Techniques of Neutralization: A Theory of Delinquency." *American Sociological Review* 22 (6): 664–670.

Tannen, Deborah. 1989. *Talking Voices: Repetition, Dialogue, and Imagery in Conversational Discourse*. Cambridge: Cambridge University Press.

Tarde, Gabriel. 1892. "Les Crimes des Foules." *Archives de l'Anthropologie Criminelle* 7:353–386.

Taylor, Charles. 1985. *Human Agency and Language: Philosophical Papers I*. Cambridge: Cambridge University Press.

Thompson, Robert S., Amy E. Bonomi, Melissa Anderson, Robert J. Reid, Jane A. Dimer, David Carrell, and Frederick P. Rivara. 2006. "Intimate Partner Violence: Prevalence, Types, and Chronicity in Adult Women." *American Journal of Preventive Medicine* 30 (6): 447–457.

Tilly, Charles. 2006. *Why?* Princeton, NJ: Princeton University Press.

Tittle, Charles R. 1995. *Control Balance: Toward a General Theory of Deviance*. Boulder, CO: Westview.

————. 2004. "Refining Control Balance Theory." *Theoretical Criminology* 8 (4): 395–428.

Tjaden, Patricia, and Nancy Thoennes. 2000. *Full Report of the Prevalence, Incidence, and Consequences of Violence against Women: Findings from the National Violence Against Women Survey.* Washington, DC: U.S. Department of Justice, Office of Justice Programs, National Institute of Justice. https://www.ncjrs.gov/pdffiles1/nij/183781.pdf.

Toby, Jackson. 1966. "Violence and the Masculine Ideal: Some Qualitative Data." *Annals of the American Academy of Political and Social Science* 364 (1): 20–27.

Tombs, Steve. 2007. "'Violence,' Safety Crimes and Criminology." *British Journal of Criminology* 47:531–550.

Tombs, Steve, and Paddy Hillyard. 2004. "Towards a Political Economy of Harm: States, Corporations and the Production of Inequality." In *Beyond Criminology: Taking Harm Seriously,* edited by Paddy Hillyard, Christina Pantazis, Steve Tombs, and Dave Gordon, 30–54. London: Pluto.

Towns, Alison, and Peter Adams. 2000. "If I Really Loved Him Enough, He Would Be Okay: Women's Accounts of Male Partner Violence." *Violence against Women* 6 (6): 558–585.

Turner, Jonathan H. 2007. "Self, Emotions, and Extreme Violence: Extending Symbolic Interactionist Theorizing." *Symbolic Interaction* 30 (4): 501–530.

United Nations General Assembly. 1948. *Convention on the Prevention and Punishment of the Crime of Genocide.* Human Rights Web. http://www.hrweb.org/legal/genocide.html.

Vandello, Joseph A., and Dov Cohen. 2003. "Male Honor and Female Fidelity: Implicit Cultural Scripts That Perpetuate Domestic Violence." *Journal of Personality and Social Psychology* 84 (5): 997–1010.

Vetlesen, Arne Johan. 2005. *Evil and Human Agency: Understanding Collective Evildoing.* Cambridge: Cambridge University Press.

Ward, Tony, and Shadd Maruna. 2007. *Rehabilitation.* London: Routledge.

Websdale, Neil. 1998. *Rural Woman Battering and the Justice System: An Ethnography.* Thousand Oaks, CA: Sage.

Weiss, Elaine. 2004. *Surviving Domestic Violence: Voices of Women Who Broke Free.* Valcano, CA: Vanano.

West, Candace, and Don H. Zimmerman. 1987. "Doing Gender." *Gender and Society* 1 (2): 125–151.

Wheatcroft, Geoffrey. 2011. "Opinion: A World in Denial of What It Knows." *New York Times,* December 31. http://www.nytimes.com/2012/01/01/opinion/sunday/unknown-knowns-avoiding-the-truth.html?pagewanted=1&_r=1.

White, Hayden. 1987. *The Content of the Form: Narrative Discourse and Historical Representation.* Baltimore: Johns Hopkins University Press.

Whorf, Benjamin Lee. 1956. "Language, Mind, and Reality." In *Language, Thought, and Reality: Selected Writings of Benjamin Lee Whorf,* edited by John B. Carroll, 246–270. Cambridge, MA: MIT Press.

Wieviorka, Michel. 2009. *Violence: A New Approach.* Translated by David Macey. London: Sage.

Wolfgang, Marvin E., and Franco Ferracuti. 1967. *The Subculture of Violence: Towards an Integrated Theory in Criminology.* London: Tavistock.

Wolf-Smith, Jane H., and Ralph LaRossa. 1992. "After He Hits Her." *Family Relations* 41 (3): 324–329.

Wood, Julia T. 2004. "Monsters and Victims: Male Felons' Accounts of Intimate Partner Violence." *Journal of Social and Personal Relationships* 21 (5): 555–576.

Wood, Linda A., and Heather Rennie. 1994. "Formulating Rape: The Discursive Construction of Victims and Villains." *Discourse and Society* 5 (1): 125–148.

Woolford, Andrew. 2006. "Making Genocide Unthinkable: Three Guidelines for a Critical Criminology of Genocide." *Critical Criminology* 14:87–106.

Yacoubian, George S. 2000. "The (In)significance of Genocidal Behavior to the Discipline of Criminology." *Crime, Law, and Social Change* 34 (1): 7–19.

Yazzie, Robert, and James W. Zion. 2003. "Navajo Restorative Justice: The Law of Equality and Justice." In *A Restorative Justice Reader: Texts, Sources, Context,* edited by Gerry Johnstone, 144–151. Cullompton, UK: Willan.

Young, Jock. 2003. "Merton with Energy, Katz with Structure: The Sociology of Vindictiveness and the Criminology of Transgression." *Theoretical Criminology* 7 (3): 389–414.

Zehr, Howard. 1995. *Changing Lenses: A New Focus for Crime and Justice.* Scottsdale, PA: Herald.

Zerubavel, Eviatar. 1997. *Social Mindscapes: An Invitation to Cognitive Sociology.* Cambridge, MA: Harvard University Press.

Index

Page numbers followed by T indicate tables.

Index

About the Author

Lois Presser is an associate professor of sociology at the University of Tennessee. She studied at Cornell University (BS 1987), Yale University (MBA 1994), and the University of Cincinnati (PhD 2002). Her research pertains to intersections of culture and harm, power, justice, and restorative justice practices. Guided by questions of creativity and constraint in social action, her work has been published in academic journals including *Justice Quarterly, Signs,* and *Social Problems.* She is also the author of *Been a Heavy Life: Stories of Violent Men* (University of Illinois Press, 2008).